The Now Factors of College Success

Jermaine M. Davis, M.A.
Nancy Hunter Denney, M.A.
Michael Miller, M.A.

Zing!
Leadership
Development Systems, LLC
Just add people.

Marion, Massachusetts

Published by Zing! Leadership Development Systems, LLC.

Cover Design by Josh Visser
Layout by Corryn Hurst and Josh Visser

All inquires should be addressed to:

Zing! Leadership Development Systems, LLC.
Box 1041
Marion, MA 02738
www.zingleadership.com
nhdenney@aol.com
508.864.4027

Library of Congress Cataloging-in-Publication Data
Davis, Jermaine M., Nancy Hunter Denney and Michael Miller
The Now Factors of College Success

ISBN-13: 978-0-9792134-4-1
ISBN-10: 0-9792134-4-4
1. College 2. Reference 3. Study Guide

Printed in the United States of America

Dedication

This book is dedicated to those who enthusiastically seek
knowledge; to those who joyfully share it; and to those
who unselfishly support the process.

The Now Factors of College Success

TABLE OF CONTENTS

Do the Math 14
Where You Fit In 18
Hang Time and Places 24
Factors of Success 26
The Urgency of Now Factors 30
College Success 36

College is Not High School – Factor One
- Invest in where you are. 42
- Believe the deadlines. 42
- Don't gossip. 44
- Write your next chapter. 44
- Make friends with different kinds of people. 45
- Discover your hidden interests. 46
- Know your *College Student Bill of Rights*. 48

Whoever Said College is the Best Four Years of Your Life Never Went – Factor Two
- Set realistic expectations. 52
- Know that to succeed also means to fail. 54
- Give yourself room to grow. 55
- Make your own mistakes then move on. 56
- Recognize you are not the only one with questions. 57

Letting Go Often Means Holding Onto Something Else – Factor Three
- Attend your orientation program. 60
- Accept the changing relationship with your parent(s) or guardian(s). 61
- Keep a journal. 63
- Get out of your room. 64
- Be willing to be alone. 65

A Roommate is Someone Who Shares Your Room – Factor Four
- Negotiate lights out time. 68
- Pick up after yourself. 68
- Never borrow things without asking. 69
- Respect one another's privacy. 70
- Learn how to be compatible. 70
- Speak up when there's a problem. 72

When You Turn Off the Technology, You Turn On the Possibilities – Factor Five
- Know how much time you spend with technology. 76
- Limit the time you spend on your cell phone. 80
- Schedule phone calls home. 80
- Treat yourself to technology down time. 81
- Have face to face conversations before jumping on Facebook. 81
- Get involved in student organizations. 82
- Attend campus events. 83
- Take advantage of campus facilities. 83

When You Take Care of Today, Tomorrow Happens – Factor Six
- Live in the present. 88
- Develop effective organizational skills. 88
- Use a daily planner. 90
- Learn to say, "No." 91
- Remove temptations or distractions. 92
- Think big picture. 94
- Attend to your space and psyche. 95
- Find ways to keep yourself motivated. 97
- Run (don't walk) away from procrastination. 98

Being Undeclared is Not Necessarily Being Undecided – Factor Seven
- Try taking a pass/fail course. 104
- Look for the telling signs. 104
- Stay in touch with your academic advisor. 106

You Will Get Higher Grades by Sitting in the Front Row – Factor Eight

- Sit in the front row of class. 110
- Learn how to learn. 110
- Read the additional reading list. 111
- Participate in classroom discussions. 112
- Ask questions when you don't understand. 112
- Pay the cost to be the boss. 113

Absence Makes the Your Grades Go Down – Factor Nine

- Go to class. 116
- Pick class times to optimize your learning. 116
- Honor your professor. 118
- Introduce yourself to your classmates. 118
- Calculate the actual dollar value of a class. 119
- Respect the rationale for attendance. 120

Turning Pages Isn't Reading – Factor Ten

- Read to teach. 124
- Allow enough time to study. 125
- Find a quiet place to read. 125
- Highlight the important things. 126
- Schedule time to re-read. 127
- Test yourself on your reading. 127

Professors are People Too – Factor Eleven

- Get to know your professors. 132
- Go to office hours. 132
- Understand your role as a student – not a consumer. 133

Cheating is When You Don't Do Your Own Work – Factor Twelve

- Know your college's academic policies. 136
- Don't take shortcuts. 138
- Avoid blaming your professors. 139
- Look for the rationale behind assignments and required courses. 140
- Put grades in perspective. 141

Character Always Counts – Factor Thirteen
- Remember wherever you go, there you are. 144
- Apologize when you are wrong. 145
- Attend leadership development opportunities. 146
- Treat others with respect. 148
- Ask yourself the tough questions. 150
- Stand up for what's right. 151

You Can be Smart and Stupid at the Same Time – Factor Fourteen
- Identify your core values and morals. 154
- Say "No!" to peer pressure. 155
- Know your limits. 156
- Drink in moderation or not at all. 157
- Respect your right (or their right) to not have sex. 158
- Don't walk around at night alone. 159
- Seek compatible and supportive relationships. 160

Love Makes the World Go Round – Factor Fifteen
- Love yourself first. 164
- Seek romantic relationships based upon mutual respect. 165
- Be there for others. 166
- Quit friendships that aren't serving you well. 167

When Your Tank is Empty You Can't Go Far – Factor Sixteen
- Recalculate your need to consume food. 172
- Stay SHARP. 173
- Focus on the positive outcomes of taking proper care of yourself. 175
- Avoid all-nighters. 177
- Ask for help when you need it. 177
- Say, "No" to being hazed or hazing others. 179
- Find sources of spiritual renewal. 181
- Talk to your resident advisor. 182

Laughter isn't Always the Best Medicine – Factor Seventeen
- Keep it all in perspective. 186
- Know your health insurance information. 187
- Schedule annual medical exams in advance. 188
- Let professors (and other important people) know when you are sick. 188

Just Because You Can Doesn't Mean You Should – Factor Eighteen
- Decide how to make decisions. 192
- Get into a healthy sleeping routine. 193
- Resist the temptation to go home every weekend. 193
- Don't spend money you don't have. 194
- Take ownership for your financial future. 195
- Look on and off campus for a job. 197
- Balance your checkbook. 198
- Start building your investment portfolio now. 199
- Go without a car. 199

College is the Real World – Factor Nineteen
- Find a mentor. 202
- Network and follow up with people. 202
- Register to vote. 203

The Future is Yours to Create – Factor Twenty
- Think beyond getting a "job." 206
- Pick a career that engages you. 206
- Visit the idea of vocation. 208
- Believe in yourself. 210

Take Care Now 214
About the Authors 216

Chapter 1

DO THE MATH

"Live as though you were going to die tomorrow; but learn as if you were going to live forever!"

Gandhi

Is a line a shape? You may not know the answer to this question, but you have a fifty percent chance of guessing correctly! There is little penalty in being wrong and aside from a fleeting moment of personal satisfaction, little reward for being right. Is a line a shape? Guess again.

As is the case with most questions, there comes a time in your life when answers are relative. Absolutes and certainties become less important. Instead of becoming more knowing and comfortable in your own skin, you wake up one day with the daunting suspicion you don't know everything. The only thing that is certain is the uncertainty (or unfamiliarity) of your surroundings. It is as if you are part of a mathematical equation with more than one correct answer.

Whether math is or isn't your thing won't affect your ability to understand a straight forward formula for college success, or hinder your ability to understand the useful factors and tips presented on the pages to follow. Formulas simply organize information making it possible to solve when "variables" change. How you solve for college success remains constant. Here's your first look at the formula created to ease your transition to official "college student."

The Formula for College Success

$$\text{College Success} = f(P + E) + \text{Now Factors}$$

Don't panic! What might appear to be overwhelming, exhausting or too much to handle, becomes an exercise in tackling smaller units – one at a time – until the entire equation has been solved. The same theory applies to the years and challenges which lay ahead of you.

According to the formula, your college success is a function of you, the person (P), in your environment (E), with the added benefit of 20 pieces of wisdom (Now Factors) which are essential observations about achieving success in college. All of the Now Factors need to be understood in order to complete the equation. You don't necessarily have to review these factors in any order, but you can't solve the entire problem (i.e. achieve college success) until you appreciate each factor. Do what you can do, when you can do it. Eventually, you will discover the answers to numerous typical, and not-so-typical, questions about how to have a successful college career.

Knowledge is power. Knowing what to expect before you find yourself in a situation without what you need can be the difference between passing or failing a course. Just ask the student who gets an "F" on his first exam and responds by going to a study skills workshop the next week. Although you might be inclined to praise his decision, the "working smarter not harder theory" encouraged in this book would suggest the value in checking out a study skills workshop prior to taking your first exam! *Now Factors* represent the knowledge you need to maximize your potential and prepare for the diverse set of challenges found on a college campus.

Did you know, for example, in college level courses the lowest grade isn't dropped or forgiven, and unlike high school or other learning environments, there may only be two or three exams for the entire course? You will be more successful in college when you anticipate typical challenges and proactively prepare for them. This is why the very first thing you should do with the Formula for College Success is plug yourself into the equation!

Did You Know?

There were 8 United States presidents who never attended college including George Washington and Abraham Lincoln.

Chapter 2

WHERE YOU FIT IN

"Your work is to discover your work, and then with all your heart to give yourself to it."

Buddha

You are a unique human being. What are the odds you'll make the same mistakes, trip over the same stumbling blocks, or fall into the same traps as those who have come before you? Believe it or not, the odds are quite high. You are different, yet not all that different. Certain generalities drawn from years of watching college students – both in and out of the classroom, suggest there are conclusions which continue to be true – year after year, and student after student.

But, you do make the equation more interesting! From your personality to the environment that shaped you, the Formula for College Success just wouldn't work without your participation. Based on the theory below, "Behavior is a function of the person interfacing with his or her environment," your college success is dependent upon how you interact in new surroundings. The Now Factors are added to the equation to offer guidance.

$$Behavior = f (Person + Environment)$$

Wherever you go... there you are! You are accompanied by how you laugh, respond to strangers, feel pain, and solve problems. With every new venue comes the likelihood you will be changed by it. From this moment on, you have the ability to create (even predict) a different outcome by appropriately adjusting to your surroundings.

Change is something you can count on. It represents one of the few constants in your world for the months and years ahead. You'll get used to becoming someone you haven't met yet. After all, you've been changing your entire life. Stuff happens. You either react or don't react, which sets you up for the next unknown. At the end of the day, it is *you* (the person) who ultimately determines your destiny.

You play a significant role in the kind of success you will have and how it will be achieved. The Formula for College Success is personal because of what you bring to it. No two formulas can be the same. Here's another look at your future…

$$\text{College Success} = f(P + E) + \text{Now Factors}$$

ASSIGNMENT: FINDING YOUR SENSE OF IDENTITY

Directions: Below is a classification of "identity markers." How would you personalize each one at this moment? To the right of each item, provide further explanation, descriptions or examples.

Identifier:

Level of self-esteem: _____
_____
_____

Sense of humor: _____
_____
_____

Degree of patience: _____
_____
_____

Ability to handle frustration: _____
_____
_____

Appreciation for diversity: _____
_____
_____

Desires: _____
_____
_____

Types of interests: _____
_____
_____

Level of maturity: _____
_____
_____

Aptitudes: _____
_____
_____

Role of spirituality in your life: _____
_____
_____

Physical conditioning: _____
_____
_____

Talents: _____
_____
_____

Outlook on life: _____
_____
_____

Intelligence: _____
_____
_____

Sense of autonomy: _____
_____
_____

Capacity for understanding: _____
_____
_____

Ability to experience joy: _____
_____
_____

A Thought About Writing Without a Pen

The above exercise required a pen. If you didn't have one, did you skip over the exercise or did you do it in your head? Did you pause and go find a pen? If not, will you remember your answers by the end of the book, or by the end of the year? You can't write without a writing implement. You can't achieve in college without the Now Factors! This is your window of opportunity. Seize it! Why not get a pen and fill in the answers above?

Did You Know?

The oldest university in the country is Harvard, established in 1636. The second oldest is the College of William and Mary, established in 1693.

Chapter 3

HANG TIME AND PLACES

"Find good cupcakes. A bad day gets better if frosting is involved."

Kaitlin Denney, student
George Washington University, Washington, D.C.

Another significant variable found in the Formula for College Success is literally where you find yourself, spend your time and hang out. This includes your immediate environment, the situations you anticipate and those that just happen. If someone were to yell as you sit reading this book, "There's a snake under your seat!" you might instinctively lift up your feet. You might scream. You might smile, and quietly lean over to see if there really was a snake under your seat. There would be a reaction. What's going on around you can't help but influence your behavior.

College is a new environment – it's not high school or taking courses online. Whether you live on campus, work two jobs or go to college part time, the more aware you are of your surroundings the more appreciative you can be of the positive influences they can have on your success. The trick is to place yourself in the right environments at the right times! Look at the different kinds of "locations" which make up the environment (E) part of the Formula for College Success.

ENVIRONMENTAL INFLUENCES:

- Campus facilities, buildings and grounds
- Level of expectations by professors, parents, staff members and peers
- Written and implied policies
- Campus traditions
- School spirit
- Standards of conduct and civility
- Religious practices and presence
- Residential life program
- Nature and wildlife on campus
- Roommate or living situation

Chapter 4

FACTORS OF SUCCESS

"Before everything else, getting ready is the secret to success."

Henry Ford

Ever bake a cake and forget to add the eggs? If you're hungry enough, you eat the cake anyway. Food is food. You've undoubtedly also downed a few bags of stale potato chips in your lifetime, swallowed a few gallons of flat soda and admit it... brushed your teeth with your fingers because you forgot your toothbrush! You had needs and found creative ways to meet them! Missing a few ingredients didn't get you down or slow you down. That can't happen now! If you are missing the knowledge of the Now Factors, you need to stop and get it. You persevered in the face of possible starvation, or worse yet... waking up to Icky Mouth Syndrome. The key to your college success is likely found in the Now Factors.

Numbers have a place. They are most useful when getting into an elevator, talking your way out of a speeding ticket, or being identified at the DMV. Numbers organize, demonstrate, quantify and tally. They bring precision, detail and in many circumstances, certainty or significance of the statistical kind. It's rather cool the way numbers don't end. They are infinite – unlike people or cats.

There are a finite number of "never fail" observations about succeeding in college – 20 to be exact. The more Now Factors you accept as truth, and the sooner, the greater your chances for college success. The role of a Now Factor is to identify an important lesson so you can learn it without discovering it for yourself. Remember being told, "Don't lick icicles with your tongue because it will stick to it," but you did it anyway? Remember being warned, "Don't put your hand on the stove top because it is still hot," but you did it anyway? You still have the scars as proof of your defiance!

Instead of getting "stuck" or "burned," stop continuing to learn some of life's tough lessons the hard way! Trust the Now Factors. Knowing them will lead you to the accomplishment of your goals and help you to be a contributing member of your learning and living communities. They will ease your transformation to "college student."

College Success = f (P + E) + Now Factors

Take another look at the equation above. You might be tempted to solve the entire equation right now. Odds are, however, you don't know what it is you don't know yet! Study the Now Factors in any order you want. Go from the back of the book and work your way forward. Do whatever it takes to understand the wisdom of rather simple observations with expediential positive power. Some are harder than others to comprehend and some are "no brainers." Others will leave you staring in the mirror while scratching your head, as if you were attempting to solve a huge polynomial equation on a blackboard, but don't have a clue. You will most likely figure all this out on your own and in good time. But why not start with an advantage?

Did You Know?

There are 57 college campuses with same mascot; the Eagles.

(Source: *College in a Can* by Sandra and Harry Choron)

Chapter 5

THE URGENCY OF NOW FACTORS

"Nothing great was ever achieved without enthusiasm."

Ralph Waldo Emerson

Some things in life simply aren't debatable or "open for discussion." There are absolutes, right and wrong answers, and "definites." The Now Factors presented in the following chapters can be thought of as "observations with attitude." Each one of them has been tested, observed over time and found to be applicable to most students on university and college campuses across the country. The sooner you make them part of your every day, the sooner you will see positive results.

You are encouraged to step up to the plate, start swinging, and begin thinking about your college success in terms of the immediate or now. Your college success may depend upon something as simple as timing. One of the most forceful negative behaviors in any life equation is *procrastination*. The Now Factors actively fight your natural-born tendency to do later that which needs your attention now!

Assignment: Delayed Gratification

Direction: Take a quick look at the following words. Which actions or mind sets lead to achievement and which will keep you standing still as the college years pass you by?

Option A	Option B
Procrastination	Perseverance
Tardy	Punctual
Waste	Value
Delay	Immediate
Indifference	Determined
Reactive	Proactive
Later	Sooner
Resistance	Diligence
Coincidence	Deliberate
Thoughts	Goals
Motionless	Movement
Distraction	Concentration
Whenever	Now!

From this moment on, you are encouraged to look at the concept of procrastination from a different perspective. Specifically, look at procrastination as an indicator of your commitment to happiness, personal achievement, growth, maturity, character development and success. Despite what you might believe, procrastination really isn't about time. It's about the vision you have for your future. When you are able to see yourself being successful in college and in life, you are more likely to make a commitment and invest in your anticipated success. You can also avoid failing by not trying. The major flaw with this logic is it also guarantees the possibility of not succeeding!

THINKING PAD

Don't put off the Now Factors. They are designed to help you get where you want to go – even if you don't know where that is yet. You have to believe *in* you in order to achieve *for* you. Take a moment and just think about how you want to be by the end of this year.

Question to Self: Where do I want to be by the end of this year?

_____

_____

_____

_____

_____

_____

_____

_____

_____

_____

_____

_____

Question to Self: How do I want to describe myself in four, five and six years from now?

_____

_____

_____

_____

_____

_____

_____

_____

_____

_____

_____

Question to Self: What is "college success" to me? How will I know what it looks like?

_____

_____

_____

_____

_____

_____

_____

_____

_____

_____

_____

Question to Self: What do I always seem to "put off" until it's too late?

_____

_____

_____

_____

_____

_____

_____

_____

_____

_____

_____

_____

Did You Know?

According to a study conducted by the College Board in 2007, a bachelor's degree holder will earn over the course of their lifetime, 60% (or close to a million dollars) more than someone with a high school diploma.

[Source: www.ehow.com]

Chapter 6

COLLEGE SUCCESS

"Man's main task in life is to give birth to himself, to become what he potentially is."

Erich Fromm

Becoming a college student is worthy of celebration, acknowledgment, pride, or at the very least, a Hallmark card from an unknown relative. Congratulations! If you are entering college or are in college, you now represent approximately 30% of the US population. Impressed or shocked? Maybe both? By all definitions of "success," you've accomplished something many Americans aren't able to achieve – getting to college! If you manage to graduate with an Associate's Degree (two year degree) or Bachelor's (four year degree), you become part of an even smaller pool of Americans. Not only do you *get into* college, you *finish*!

There are advantages and correlated positive behaviors associated with individuals who have a college degree compared to those who do not. Did you know according to College Board (2010), higher levels of education are correlated to the following:

- lower smoking rates
- more positive perceptions of personal health
- lower rate of imprisonment
- higher levels of civic participation
- more involvement in volunteer work
- higher voter turn out rate
- higher blood donors
- lower unemployment rates
- greater earning potential (typically college graduates earn 60% more than high school graduates)

As Americans we grow up believing, "We are number one!" Ever wonder in what? If we were all to be honest, the only thing you really can claim with all certainty is your effort to be the very best you. Are you going to give 100% to becoming number one, or less than everything you've got? What does it mean to be "number one" to you?

College is designed to make you different, so if you come out differently than you went in, was it a win? The key is to understand from the beginning what college is about; look beyond "getting a diploma" as the single measurement of your efforts. Thomas Jefferson, one of higher education's founding fathers noted, "The foremost goal of American education must be to nurture the natural aristocracy of talent and virtue." He is suggesting college success is achieved when you graduate with improved skills, intelligence, values, morals, and competencies. For Jefferson, reaching for your untapped potential in order to enhance society defines "college success." What do you think?

As the Formula for College Success implies, college is more than studying for exams, going to class and doing homework. Yes, it's more than getting a diploma. College is the ultimate "laboratory of learning" across many dimensions of growth. It's a place to exchange and create ideas, think critically, and be curious.

TIME TO EXPLORE

In the chapters to follow, you will be given numerous opportunities to explore how you think and feel about specific topics related to college success. These thought provoking activities are labeled, "Assignments." They come in the form of lists, poems, fill-in-the-blank exercises, word associations, questions, and blank lines for your more "random" thoughts. You can decide to play along, jump in when you are in a better mood, or not participate. Whatever you do is up to you; as is what you decide to not do. It will be more helpful, however, to complete as many of your "assignments" as possible because they are crafted to make you think!

Offered as one consistent "whack on the side of your head," are the sections identified as "Thinking Pad." Questions will be asked that only *you* can answer. After you let each question percolate in your head, take a moment to record your answer. What doesn't make sense to you today may be easier to figure out down the road.

ASSIGNMENT: MY DEFINITION OF COLLEGE SUCCESS

Directions: Take a look at the list of potential areas of growth and experiences. Place check marks next to the goals (or potential outcomes of attending college) which appeal to you and a line through those you've already achieved. You will soon discover "success" is achieved in bits and pieces.

_____ Grow up.

_____ Become someone I value.

_____ Figure out what it means to be me.

_____ Do my laundry without turning my clothes pink.

_____ Handle adversity with grace.

_____ Take responsibility for my actions.

_____ Establish relationships founded in trust.

_____ Take advantage of opportunities for involvement.

_____ Appreciate the value of diversity over tolerating differences.

_____ Become more accepting of others and less judgmental.

_____ Think.

_____ Learn to prioritize what matters most.

_____ Explore vocational opportunities and possible career paths.

_____ Control my emotions.

_____ Accurately express myself to strangers.

_____ Communicate effectively to get my needs met.

_____ Avoid spending what I don't have.

_____ Save money.

_____ Grow in my faith or spirituality.

_____ Learn from my successes and my failures.

_____ Befriend my elders.

_____ Learn to respect those with life experience.

_____ Channel my energies towards productive and positive endeavors.

_____ Use my time well.

_____ Have pride in my college.

_____ Establish mentoring relationships.

_____ Laugh.

_____ Contribute to my living and learning community.

_____ Expand my understanding of different cultures and parts of the world.

_____ Get smarter.

_____ Find my creative and innovative side.

_____ Learn to forgive others and myself.

_____ Grow in my moral reasoning.

_____ Learn what it means to be ethical and act with integrity.

_____ Help others achieve their goals.

_____ Support campus activities, sporting events, cultural series, and so on.

_____ Leave my fingerprints for the better on my alma mater.

_____ Become more comfortable in my own shoes.

_____ Play by the rules.

_____ Treat others with respect, as I'd like to be treated.

_____ Change.

What needs to be added to your list of "college success" outcomes?

_____

_____

_____

_____

_____

_____

_____

"Think like a wise man
but communicate in the
language of the people."

- William Butler Yeats

Random Thoughts...

Chapter 7

NOW FACTOR ONE

COLLEGE IS NOT HIGH SCHOOL

"You have to leave the city of your comfort and go into the wilderness of your intuition. What you'll discover will be wonderful. What you'll discover will be yourself."

Alan Alda

INVEST IN WHERE YOU ARE.

If you "invest" in your learning and growth, there is an automatic return on your investment. Simply put, your commitment of time and energy are not wasted because the benefits are personal. What you put in, determines what you will take out of this experience. Those who "spend time" in college versus those who "invest" in their education, typically attend because they were told, "You are going to college!" You have to *want* to be in college to sustain the motivation needed to succeed.

College is more than the *act* of "showing up." The paradigm has shifted! The "currency" of your education is different than what you've previously experienced. As a college student, you "pay" by being where you need to be, even if you don't see the immediate value. You contribute in class by raising your hand, even if you might be nervous. You re-write your class notes, even if you can almost decipher the scribble! If nothing is invested in the first place, little "interest" is earned.

BELIEVE THE DEADLINES.

It's worth repeating: Not all things in life are debatable. In college, when time is up, it's usually up; and when something is due, that's when it's due. Whether you are able to meet a deadline or not isn't going to be your professor's problem; it's going to be your problem.

If you are a traditionally aged student, you're probably familiar with taking standardized tests and understand the rigidity of test taking and scoring. Because laws have been passed to ensure different learning situations are taken into consideration, you might be among those who were given more time, or special accommodations when taking standardized tests. It's also possible you were able to "negotiate" an extended deadline now and again with a classroom teacher or received a "pass" on a project for one reason or another. As a college student, don't assume (or expect) a college professor will be so understanding. Ask each of your professors about their classroom policies and know your syllabus.

To avoid receiving a failing grade – or no credit at all for your efforts, respect your professor's deadlines and time parameters. It is well within his or her rights to hold you accountable for handing in a paper after the due date .They can refuse it altogether, or lower your score by a grade. Locking you out of class if you're late, collecting your exam paper before you've finished, or not allowing you to make up a pop quiz from a skipped or missed class, are all fair game.

How do you learn what's fair game and all of the unwritten rules? The best way is to establish an close relationship with your course syllabus the very first day of class. Take it to lunch. Every course you take will have a *syllabus* (Latin term meaning *label*.) It outlines the expectations, requirements, dates of exams, and deadlines for projects. Commonly, your syllabus also explains the grading system for that particular course. Be sure to check the class attendance requirement in each syllabi… showing up to class is often a requirement for passing the class!

As in any long lasting relationship, treat your course syllabus with respect! Don't toss it away after you've reviewed it. Place it in your course notebook. The serious students will go as far as to cover it in plastic to protect it from damage! Exam dates and deadlines in each course syllabus should be copied into your daily planner. Keep in mind, however, your professors may alter these dates. Why? Because they can.

Don't gossip.

You are in college to grow, learn new things, and think about how you can make the world a better place. Regardless of your age, behaviors such as gossiping quickly diminish your character and perceived level of maturity by others. Instead of strengthening your potential to learn things about the people around you, speaking about others for the sake of spreading rumors, takes up precious air time.

Move forward, onward and upward! When in conversations with others, keep the focus on those present – not on those absent from the opportunity to contribute, or as the unfortunate case may be, correct the script of a play to which they have the starring role due to their obvious absence.

If the conversation goes south – despite your efforts to keep it real, stand up for being straight up.

How do you stop the gossip? Respond with statements of maturity, "I'm not comfortable with this topic, let's talk about you." Then, ask a question about the other people who *are* present. People like to talk about themselves. Talking about others for the sake of talking about others (unless it's all positive, of course) is immature and mean.

Write your next chapter.

Everyone – including you – starts with a clean slate, so write on it well. Aside from those one or two former classmates, or familiar faces from your hometown Starbucks, most new students (or transfers) are essentially unknown entities. You are a complete stranger to your classmates, and in almost all cases, to your roommates. Sure, you might know *about* your roommates, Facebooked each other over the summer, but you don't really *know* them. They don't really know you either. This fact shouldn't be frustrating or make you feel alone – it should be freeing!

Freedom. As a college student, you get to create a "new and improved" version of you. Every day, make a decision to turn off those unhealthy, immature or unproductive behaviors from your past, and replace them with better ones. For example, if you are a smoker, consider quitting. When you put down this book, make a commitment to seek the help you need to put down the cigarettes. Smoking in college doesn't hold the same perceived social status it did in high school – just the opposite. You will be required to smoke 100 feet from any building and never in residence halls, academic buildings, or any facility on campus. Students who don't particularly care for the smell of smoke will move away from you in lecture halls. Why not decide to be seen as a more health conscious individual and start running every morning? Here are a few more examples...

If you weren't into doing your own work in previous years, stop cheating and start allowing yourself more preparation for exams and assignments. Others will see you as a person with integrity. If you were formally known as a "party animal" and suffered the consequences, no one needs to know that about you, unless you tell them. Bragging about being a "heavy drinker" isn't all that impressive to college students interested in being successful. If you want to seek more genuine ways of building a social circle of true friends, consider joining a student organization or attending a few of the many non-alcohol related functions offered on campus. Why not become someone of enhanced character?

MAKE FRIENDS WITH DIFFERENT KINDS OF PEOPLE.

If you find yourself surrounded by people who seem to have been born on a different planet and raised by aliens, don't panic. Be patient. They might just become your best friends!

College is a wonderful place to meet a diversity of individuals you normally wouldn't seek out and befriend. Connected by similar challenges and daily experiences, the many "strangers" around you really aren't all that strange, they are merely different than you. This is a good thing.

Diversity comes in all shapes, sizes and colors. It offers a gift of personal awareness to other cultures, the opportunity to learn how to seek common understandings, and a unique chance to become more open minded, knowledgeable and enlightened. As you begin to build your "life's social network," ask yourself where else you would have the opportunity to build such diverse friendships and potentially lasting relationships with people who will show you the world, by showing you themselves.

By the way, if someone appears strange to you, don't doubt you may also appear weird to them. All you really are to each other is new. Introduce yourself. Seek the common ground by recognizing you are both at the same place at the same time. Before you judge or dismiss someone, ask yourself, "What would I like this person to know about me and what do I really want to know about them?"

DISCOVER YOUR HIDDEN INTERESTS.

There is so much you really don't know about yourself, let alone the strangers around you. Beneath the external you is a mystery of great magnitude waiting to be discovered.

Trial and error is not always pretty, but it gets the job done. The college and university community is rich in opportunities to explore your hidden talents, interests, desires, and dreams. When you give something new a shot, you literally expand your base of life experiences and *increase* the odds you'll impress yourself. When you play it safe and go with what you know, you *decrease* the probability of achieving the many positive items on your list of desired outcomes from college. It's a numbers game.

ASSIGNMENT: OPPORTUNITIES FOR DISCOVERY

Directions: There are literally hundreds, even thousands, of opportunities for getting in touch with those things you are – or might be – passionate about. The opportunities for self-discovery below might end up surprising you in many ways! Place a check mark next to a few that interest you.

_____ Attend a campus musical performance.

_____ Take a ball room dance class.

_____ Maximize your "elective" course options by taking an art class.

_____ Join one or two student organizations.

_____ Attend a guest lecture.

_____ Participate in a club sport.

_____ Join the Black Student Organization, even if you aren't African American.

_____ Turn off your TV (or technology) and start writing in a journal.

_____ Run for a leadership position.

_____ Befriend people completely different than you.

_____ Participate in Spring Break community service efforts.

_____ Travel abroad.

THINKING PAD

Question to Self: What kinds of things have I always been interested in that I should explore now?

_____

_____

_____

_____

_____

_____

_____

_____

KNOW YOUR COLLEGE STUDENT BILL OF RIGHTS.

Some things are simple. Truth is truth. The world is round. You matter. Despite how it might feel at times, you are more than a number! You are a human being who is also a college student. You have the right to maximize this opportunity by speaking up for yourself and asking for what you need.

The _College Bill of Rights_ is a detailed collection of realistic expectations held by college students across the country. You may often have to assert yourself to protect these rights, but they are _your_ rights to protect!

College Student Bill of Rights

- Nancy Hunter Denney

As a college student, I have the right to:

Acceptance, celebration, dignity, respect, & freedom of expression.
Say "No!" to fear, beer, and peer pressure.
Say "I don't understand."
Be "undeclared" and change my major as many times as I want.
Discover who I am when I find out.
Not know where I'm at until I get there.

Love myself when I least deserve it.
Admit "I was wrong" and move on.
Wait until I'm in love or married to make love.
Take care of my mind, spirit, and body.
Exercise regularly.
Not drink or drink in moderation.
Quit smoking or never start.

As a college student, I have the right to:

Establish friendships with people different than me.
Be a member of a civil community.
Celebrate diversity.
Dress for class in a manner reflective of my love for learning.
Love learning.
Arrive early to class and leave late.
Sit in the front row of class.
Never miss a day of class and befriend my professors.
Read every page of the "additional reading list."
Ask questions in class (except for "Will this be on the test?")

As a college student, I have the right to:

Have priorities other than my education (i.e. children…)
Disagree with – yet respect – my elders.
Become smarter, less ignorant, and more open minded.
Do the right thing with honesty and integrity.
Not allow someone to copy my work.

Join any student organization.
Know how my tuition is spent.
Get my money's worth.
Spend my time getting healthier, smarter, and more fit.
Be the small fish in the big pond.
Grow up while bringing back the child in me.

As a college student, I have the right to:

Value the privilege of higher education.
Know "boredom is not a state of mind, boredom is the state of not using your mind."

Appreciate the cost of higher education knowing the price of ignorance.
Celebrate the freedom that comes with my degree.
Create my future while becoming someone different.

Therefore, let me go. Let me discover my potential. Let me find myself in college.

Chapter 8

NOW FACTOR TWO

WHOEVER SAID "COLLEGE IS THE BEST FOUR YEARS OF YOUR LIFE" NEVER WENT

"A goal of the college experience is for students to increase the space in which they stand."

Hollie Ingraham, Director of Student Life (retired)
University of Maine at Farmington

SET REALISTIC EXPECTATIONS.

Where to begin? Ahh... at the senior prom. Is there any other event in history where anticipation far outweighs the event itself? Maybe you fit into the small majority whose date (if you had one) didn't dance with everyone else's date, or who managed to escape the drama of a gym (or hotel ballroom) filled with superficial compliments followed by backstabbing comments.

It's not that proms are bad things; they just don't have the juice to live up to the hype. The gap between great expectations and the event itself is just too great! Apply this same logic to the phrase, "College is the best four years of your life."

How can that be? Unless you've done college before, you've never done this before! It's all new. It's all different. It's all a tad scary. The overriding goal of education is to change you by presenting challenge after challenge. Trials and tribulations come with frustration and hard work. Being realistic will make all the good (and great) times seem like a bonus!

When defining "the best" always consider the source! Your professors, parents, guardians, resident advisors, coaches, campus administrators, and all others trying to provide you with an education, will most likely have a completely different definition of "the best" than you! Educators would say, "the best" four years is when you are...

- Having the opportunity to experience success and failure
- Establishing positive relationships with people different than you – whether you want to or not
- Acknowledging a shift in what matters most in life
- Learning life isn't always fair
- Experiencing the toughest lesson: bad things happen to good people

- Standing on your own two feet
- Being held accountable
- Realizing independence comes with responsibility
- Learning to think critically

College students, however, might just say "the best" four years is...

- Meeting new people with similar interests
- Staying up all night because you can
- Having multiple social opportunities and fun things to do
- Exploring new places
- Not having someone telling you what to do and when to do it

Throughout your college years, give yourself a reality check by accepting how difficult it might be for you to find your way, balance work and school, get along with roommates (if you have them), or prepare for college-level course work. College is hard. Making new friends is hard. Learning to learn is hard. Adjusting to a new routine is hard. Trying to work, study and have a relationship is hard. There will also be good times, maybe even great times. You will laugh, cry, and eventually find your way.

No one gets a crystal ball, so the best prediction of how productive your college experience actually is or is not, will be to ask yourself at the end of every day, "What did I learn about myself today?"

KNOW THAT TO SUCCEED ALSO MEANS TO FAIL.

You've heard examples throughout your lifetime of highly successful inventors, scholars, politicians, and athletes, who failed big time before "making it." Consider these examples:

- Louisa May Alcott was told by an editor that she could never write anything with popular appeal.
- Louis Pasteur was called, "a mediocre" chemistry student at the Royal College, his alma mater.
- Walt Disney was fired by a local newspaper because he didn't have any "good ideas."
- Beethoven's music teacher said that Ludwig was "hopeless" as a composer.

Failure. It happens. Unless you are the exception to the rule, failure is going to happen during your college experience – as it should. Achieving individuals learn from missing their mark, making a bad judgment call, acting immaturely, or being just plain stupid. All these help you to grow up, gain personal insight and learn what it takes to dust yourself off and try again. They teach you what *not* to do. Achieving individuals also know if you risk success you may succeed or you may fail, but if you don't even try you have failed.

Thinking Pad

Question to Ask: When did I make a mistake or fail, yet ended up better because of it?

_____
_____
_____
_____
_____
_____
_____
_____
_____

Give yourself room to grow.

How far is too far? Remember the curiosity inspired by a single rubber band during high school study hall? Merely holding it in your hands wasn't enough. This thin string of elastic dares you to wrap it around your thumb and pointer finger, quickly find an unsuspecting target, and fire! If you get too ambitious, you run the risk of taking your own eye out. Your decision... definitely worth the risk.

How far is *too* far when it comes to maximizing your potential for personal growth and achievement, finding yourself, or trying a new life experience? You will know when college is "in focus" when it goes "out of focus." Allow room for the unknown. Give yourself some slack for not knowing everything all at once. Make sense out of what you can, and store the other information until you are in a position to process it more clearly. Take inventory of what is working and what behaviors seem to consistently get you in trouble. Do more of what works.

To avoid "taking someone's eye out (including your own)" ask yourself the following questions – right now:

"What have I learned?"
"What triggered my positive reaction?"
"What is making me happy?"
"What keeps tripping me up?"
"How am I selling myself short?"
"Is there more I could be doing?"
"Am I being all that I can be?"
"How can I raise my expectations?"

MAKE YOUR OWN MISTAKES THEN MOVE ON.

Nothing is worse than getting blamed for something you didn't do, other than, not getting the credit for your perfectly executed prank, idea or "slam!" Give credit where credit is due… right? Does this mean taking ownership for the consequences of all of your choices? Affirmative.

From this moment on, consider the reality no one can make your mistakes for you. No one can (or should) fix what you broke, destroyed or dropped. If you don't hand in course assignments, wear a coat in 20 degree below zero weather, or send a birthday card to your 100-year-old grandmother, you get to accept the likelihood of a lower grade, head cold and missed opportunity to mark a special occasion. No one else gets to take the blame, feel sick or be ashamed of their own lack of consideration but the person who owns it… you!

With the ownership of your mistakes comes a greater sense of control over your destiny. It's your present. It's your future. You can take into consideration advice from parents, peer pressure, or words of caution from friends, but ultimately you will have to take responsibility for your actions. You will have to accept any consequences, and forgive or praise yourself. College is real life. You will be held accountable by others, and you need to hold yourself accountable.

Moving on from your mistakes usually depends upon the impact they had on others or the extent of negative personal consequences. What did your mistake cost? Check which of the following strategies below would keep you moving in the right direction.

WAYS TO MOVE ON AFTER MISTAKES:

- Apologize to those you negatively affected.
- Write down your mistake in a journal and what it taught you.
- If comfortable, say a prayer for forgiveness.
- Take yourself to a quiet place and come up with a plan for making a wrong right.
- Write a letter to yourself,
- Go for a run or walk.
- Completely remove yourself from the environment to a place that brings you joy.
- Seek out a positive person to spend a few hours with and share your thoughts.
- Go talk to someone in your counseling center.
- Light a candle, think about your mistake, and when you blow it out, decide to move on.

RECOGNIZE YOU ARE NOT THE ONLY ONE WITH QUESTIONS.

When you look around, does it appear everyone else is having more fun than you are? Do your fellow classmates laugh more than you do, have lots more friends and fit right in? No. It just looks that way. Most new students share more in common than they realize. What you often believe to be somebody else's reality is actually much closer to your own reality, especially when it comes to the kinds of questions you have during your college career.

As you look at the list of questions below, place a check next to those which are currently relevant. In the months ahead, re-visit this list. Odds are your choices will have changed!

QUESTIONS ABOUT COLLEGE:

_____ Will I fit in?

_____ Do I really like my friends?

_____ Am I smart enough to handle college-level work?

_____ What if I can't get along with my roommate or
          housemate?

_____ How will I know what I want to do for the rest of my life?

_____ Am I going to be OK?

_____ Are (is) my parent(s) or guardian(s) going to be OK while
          I'm in college?

_____ Can I handle a job and college?

_____ Can I really afford to be here?

_____ When will I feel like I am part of this community?

_____ Did I make the right college choice?

_____ What will become of my high school relationships?

_____ Will my friends from home stay in touch?

_____ Can my siblings make it without me?

_____ Will my classmates be way smarter than me?

Chapter 9

NOW FACTOR THREE

LETTING GO OFTEN MEANS HOLDING ONTO SOMETHING ELSE

"Everyone is so friendly the first few days of Freshmen year. Use this time to meet as many people as you can."

Josh Neuroth, student
The University of Toledo, Ohio

Attend your orientation program.

Too cool for school… not. Maybe smiling upperclassmen wearing the same bright colored shirts, leading you from one forced social interaction and small group meeting to another, isn't your thing. Maybe you want to have one more weekend home with your girlfriend or buddies. Maybe the thought of jumping in with both feet is totally overwhelming. There are lots of reasons not to attend your orientation program; yet, there are more reasons to go!

Your college orientation program (new student or transfer) is designed to introduce you to unfamiliar territory, expose you to timely resources, and assist you in meeting your classmates, faculty, and college community. Often accompanied by a catchy theme, orientation also serves to reduce any anxiety or fears around "fitting in" by offering various social events, community building activities, and advising opportunities. Just having a few extra days to find your way around campus before classes start can be the difference between being calm or nervous in your new environment.

What is an "OL?"

They come with different names or letters. Your "Orientation Leader," "Community Assistant," or "Orientation Assistant" are well trained upperclassmen committed to helping you through the transition period from "not a college student" to "college student." They have "been there" and "done that." Trained to welcome you and provide accurate answers to your questions, your "OL," "CA," or "OA," is there for you. Ask them anything you want. They will help keep it real.

Accept the changing relationship with your parent(s) or guardian(s).

It's amazing. Whoever has previously been your "authority figure" (whether a grandparent, step parent, foster parent, relative, biological parent, or combination of these), may miraculously begin to show enhanced signs of intelligence during your college years. Their advice on life, provided unselfishly over the years, may suddenly have merit. Those you once thought spoke to hear themselves talk, might come to warrant your respect and appreciation. What changed? Might the better question be, "Who changed?"

As you begin to take care of yourself and figure out how to get there from here, it's common to step out of a world where you were the sole inhabitant and realize there were many people who played a role in getting you to this place. You will know you are maturing when your relationships with those who have been invested in your life begin to be characterized by the following:

- Conversations about your future where you freely express what you want without seeking their approval or permission.
- Enhanced sense of appreciation by you for the sacrifices and support made by others (even if minimal) so you could advance your education.
- Increased desire to spend time together without any hidden or obvious agendas on your part (i.e. getting your laundry done, receiving money, borrowing the car, etc.)
- Increased diversity of conversational topics shifting from "your immediate world" to world events, politics, mutual interests and even, what is going on in their world.
- Enhanced desire to carry your own weight – pitching in around the house when visiting (i.e. taking out the trash without being asked, setting the table, being considerate of others, not

eating an entire week's worth of groceries in one night, or declining friend's invitations to go out to stay home with those so excited you are there.)

Regardless of your age, this is an amazing time to grow in your relationship with the adults in your life. As you shift from being dependent upon others to being more self-reliant, you can hold onto all the love and support you've received while letting go of the need to be "taken care of" or having decisions made *for* you, instead of *by* you.

ASSIGNMENT: CHANGING RELATIONSHIPS

Directions: To further demonstrate how relationships can change, next to each type of relationship below, identify people who would describe you as the following:

Independent:_____

Dependent:_____

Self-reliant:_____

Emerging:_____

Immature:_____

Maturing:_____

Needy:_____

KEEP A JOURNAL.

Some of the best conversations you'll ever have in college will be when no one else is around! The art of talking to yourself guarantees you'll never be without companionship, and you'll always have someone who agrees with you. Just don't get caught! People will often say things to themselves when they think no one else is listening because it's safe, free from judgment, completely honest and void of any "filters." Self-talk suggests a shift from needing others' opinions to counting more on your own. The only downside of talking to yourself is you might not remember what you said.

Keeping a journal is a means to enhanced self-understanding. It gives you a place to do any or all of the following:

- Talk about people behind their backs (or more specifically, record how you feel about those in your world and why you feel that way about them.)
- Ask open ended questions.
- Reflect upon your changing environment.
- Record special events or memorable moments of achievement.
- Brag to yourself.
- Pay yourself a few well deserved compliments or self-affirming statements.
- Make lists of your dreams, goals or desires.
- Collect inspiring quotes and words of wisdom.

For as little as one dollar, not only can you get a double cheeseburger from McDonalds, but you can get a book with blank pages from any Dollar Store to use as a "journal." You can also use your laptop. But there's something personal about being able to take a book with you to a quiet place and write your thoughts or ask questions. Here are examples of helpful questions to write in your journal. You can ask (and answer) them many times:

What am I feeling?
What triggered how I am feeling?
What am I doing to build my character this week?
How did I use my time productively today?
What brought me joy today?
Where did I fall short in living up to my personal expectations today?
How can I improve upon a relationship with _____?
What was my greatest mistake today?
How do I move forward?

GET OUT OF YOUR ROOM.

One of the most uncomfortable feelings for a college student is loneliness. Despite being in a crowd, you might still feel a sense of isolation. When you are in a new environment or wrapped up in your own world, it's not uncommon to feel as if you are the only one going through it. If you were to open up, instead of quiet down, you'd notice how many other people around you are experiencing the same feelings. This is called "transition."

When you force yourself to get out of your room and participate in your orientation program, residence hall socials, or activities fair, it becomes obvious how *not* fitting in actually *is* fitting in! It may be scary to venture out into the unknown by yourself, so consider looking for someone else who might just be waiting (or hoping) someone like you will ask them to do something. Go knock on a "stranger's" door and say, "Hey, want to check out this place with me?" Despite the security of staying connected to hometown friends, make some new friends face to face.

BE WILLING TO BE ALONE.

Although it's incredibly important to get out of your room (or leave your house or apartment) there are some moments during your college experience when solitude can calm you down and help you de-stress. Being alone for a few hours can quiet a rather noisy and hectic day.

If being alone isn't something you do well, college is a good time to practice. Solitude allows you moments of reflection and peace. It offers a chance to "de-brief" and relax. Being "on" all the time is stressful; take a breather, give yourself some space, and "retreat" to a peaceful place on campus. You will be rewarded with internal calmness. That's a good thing.

To be alone in a room and love the company is a wonderful goal. Being content with the process of "finding yourself" and being able to chill out without feeling "left out" is a sign of self-confidence and maturity. If you begin to sense "stimulus overload," back away for an hour or more. Take yourself to a movie, grab a good book, or go to the library for a quiet evening alone.

"When I was 17 I couldn't believe how much my parents didn't know. When I graduated from college, I was amazed at how much they had learned in only 7 years."

- Mark Twain

Random Thoughts...

Chapter 10

NOW FACTOR FOUR

A ROOMMATE IS SOMEONE WHO SHARES YOUR ROOM

"Perhaps the most valuable result of all education is the ability to make yourself do the thing you have to do when it ought to be done, whether you like it or not; it is the first lesson that ought to be learned; and however early a man's training begins, it is probably the last lesson that he learns thoroughly."

Thomas Huxley

NEGOTIATE LIGHTS OUT TIME.

"Negotiate lights out time" sounds like a rather obvious course of action between apartment mates or roommates, right? Yet here it is because this simple advice is frequently overlooked. Getting the right amount of sleep and privacy varies from individual to individual; making compromise and negotiation are essential.

For example, if you want to be in bed by midnight because you have an 8 a.m. class, and your roommate's first class isn't until noon you have conflicting agendas. To avoid arguments, sit down at the beginning of the year, and discuss rules around sleep, wake, and nap time. Don't assume you will know what is and isn't working for someone else's health and wellness. Some people need more sleep, and when you are inconsiderate of this fact, you get a cranky roommate!

Try to find the middle ground in your "negotiations." Get a room calendar (place it behind your door) and go night by night. Identify who has upcoming exams, early morning classes and so on. Then come to an agreement on when it will be lights out. If all this sounds ridiculous, wait until you have dark circles under your eyes and look like a raccoon! Your room is the only place on campus where you or your roommate(s) can sleep. There are other places to study, socialize and talk on the phone!

PICK UP AFTER YOURSELF.

The greatest thing about being away from home is no one is telling you to clean up your stuff! If you and your roommate(s) happen to have the same habits around cleanliness and tidiness, you won't have any problems when you trip over each other's shoes trying to find a text book. But, if one prefers to live in a clean and tidy environment, makes their bed every day, and doesn't like the smell of three-day-old pizza, remember the rule:

Being neat takes priority over being sloppy.

Having a sense of order to your life is important. When your living environment is organized and clean, it will give you a feeling of being in control. There won't be any strange odors coming from your room, and you won't be embarrassed to invite someone you've just met over for a visit. Whether you've made your own bed in the past isn't relevant. Today, it matters that you respect the fact that more than one person is living in a small space and keeping it picked up is a sign of maturity.

Do you really want to be known as "the slob" by those in your living community? You can turn over a new leaf and once a week, spend time doing laundry, cleaning your room and getting yourself organized for the week.

NEVER BORROW THINGS WITHOUT ASKING.

If it's not yours, don't use it! Even if your roommate or apartment mate, "might not" mind, don't risk taking something of theirs without asking first. There is very little you can call your own when living in a residence hall or off-campus apartment. You are sharing a space. Your "stuff" symbolizes more than material things. Your possessions identify you and help you connect with home.

The best way to avoid any problems is to not borrow each other's things. What do you do if something gets broken or stolen? What happens when a piece of clothing gets ripped? Who has to replace an item that someone else trashes? If you have it in your possession, you are responsible for its loss or damage. You need to replace it or get it fixed. You are entitled to say, "I'd prefer if you didn't use my things."

Respect one another's privacy.

When you live with someone you will know things about them and see them in ways others will not. Often, things will be said to you in confidence or with the assumption you won't be sharing the information with everyone on the floor. If you want your privacy respected, you will have to refrain from sharing personal information about your roommate(s).

Things that make up "personal information" include conversations where your roommate came into the room to be away from others. Because you live there, you weren't asked to leave. However, this doesn't mean you can share the contents of the conversation. Another example of "personal information" deals with personal hygiene, medications and health issues. It's no one else's business that your roommate sleeps with a mouth guard, or takes a prescription for her acne. By respecting each other's privacy, you are demonstrating your desire to have a relationship based upon mutual trust and positive regard.

It should go without saying (but we couldn't help ourselves) that you never have the right to go through someone else's things when they aren't present or didn't give you permission. Remember going to a friend's house and checking their medicine cabinet? Curiosity got the best of you? Refrain from "browsing" or "surfing" through your roommate's drawers, desk, and computer. Never read or open their mail. If they are having a personal conversation, give them some space. Respecting other's privacy communicates how you want your privacy to be protected!

Learn how to be compatible.

Your college roommates do not have to be in your wedding party. Although it would be nice if it works out this way, in most cases it doesn't. Your goal as a roommate is to be compatible!

Learn how to live together, don't worry about being best buddies or friends. That may or may not happen.

Roommates are often assigned by a lottery or based upon a compatibility form you completed. Does that really seem like the most effective way of ensuring success? Roommate conflicts are typical. Roommate conflicts are common. It's not easy to live with anyone let alone a complete stranger, especially if you grew up having your own room.

Most likely, you have never done this roommate thing before, so give your self some slack. Instead of telling everyone else about how it's not working out (including your parents), spend that energy working it out with your roommate(s). Come up with the "rules of compatibility" around some (or all) of the issues which typically end up presenting problems if not discussed in advance.

THINGS TO NEGOTIATE:

- Lights out time
- Cleanliness of room
- Having friends visit
- Eating in the room
- Temperature of room
- Borrowing each other's things
- Cell phone use
- Solving disputes
- Security of possessions
- Keeping confidences
- Space for storage
- Decorations

Speak up when there's a problem.

At the end of your rope? Had enough of the college living and learning community? If this is the first time you have lived away from home, expect it will be difficult – it only looks like everyone else is doing it better than you. They are not. The comforts of home or the familiarity of your former living situation is gone; replaced with something new and different.

When you are having trouble making your roommate situation work, you don't have to go it alone. There are many people trained and committed to helping you work things out. The best way to begin is with your roommate(s) or those you are having difficulty with (like the room across the hall that always plays music when you are ready for bed!) Be an adult and speak directly to the person(s) who can make the problem go away or can work with you to find a mutually agreeable solution.

If you've tried with your roommate(s) and still find yourself frustrated, or feel as if you aren't being heard, there are other options. Start with your "RA," then your "RD." The last people to consider involving are your parents or guardians. They are not the ones with the roommate problem – you are! They should not be calling your resident advisor, the mother of your roommate, or the office of residence life. Unless you feel you are in danger, or your living mates are engaged in illegal activity, it is up to you (as a college student) to attempt to resolve your conflicts.

How to Resolve Roommate Conflicts:

- Speak directly to your roommate(s).
- Talk to your resident advisor.
- Go see your resident director or someone in residential life.
- Ask a friend to go with you to negotiate living arrangements.
- Seek resources on "getting along with your roommates."

- Visit the counseling center, and speak to a professional counselor.
- Stop in the dean of students office, and ask to speak with someone.
- Talk to an upperclassman, and ask how they resolved their issues.
- Take a deep breath.
- Consider a "road trip" with a friend to get some distance and perspective.

Did You Know?

The number of students entering college (up to age 19) in 2017 is projected to be 4.2 million, according to the Department of Education.

[Source: *National Center for Education Statistics*]

"Good communication is as stimulating as black coffee and just as hard to sleep after."

- Anne Morrow Lindbergh

Random Thoughts...

Chapter 11

NOW FACTOR FIVE

WHEN YOU TURN OFF THE TECHNOLOGY, YOU TURN ON THE POSSIBILITIES

"Always have the courage to be yourself. This means doing what feels right for you; whether refusing a beer at a party, asking your roommate to turn down his loud music, or going to the library when none of your friends are studying. In college, when you follow your heart, you will meet with success."

Dr. Jennifer Duffy, Assistant Professor of Higher Education Administration
Suffolk University, Boston, Massachusetts

KNOW HOW MUCH TIME YOU SPEND WITH TECHNOLOGY.

Modern devices bring the world to your fingertips. You can access information in seconds and multi-task out of habit. Who can't write a paper, text a friend and check emails, all at the same time? Technology is intended to make your life easier, right? This theory falls short when it takes longer to fix the paper jam in your printer than it took to type the entire paper! When you get into a car accident because you were texting while driving, technology begins to cost not only time, but money.

Technology turns on the possibilities only when you use it correctly. The challenge is to learn how to harness it during college so you can use its awesome power to create more time in your life and produce a better quality of work. Technology also brings you incredible access to information and literally puts the world at your fingertips.

Technology should serve you and be used appropriately. Be careful about the misplaced priority given to your electronic games, texting, checking Facebook, surfing the web and shopping online. These activities waste valuable time technology is supposed to give you back. Take a moment to reflect on common technologies and how to use technology's incredible reach to your advantage.

ASSIGNMENT: TECHNOLOGY AND MY TIME

Directions: Take a moment to reflect on common technologies listed below. Record the amount of time you spend using each, how accessible it is to you, and how it contributes to your success – or how it might get in the way! Think about whether your time needs to be used differently.

Type of Technology:	Hours I Use it Each Day:	Accessible to me:

CELL PHONE _____   Always Sometimes Rarely

How it helps me be successful: _____

_____

How it gets in the way: _____

_____

LAPTOP COMPUTER _____   Always Sometimes Rarely

How it helps me be successful: _____

_____

How it gets in the way: _____

_____

DESK TOP COMPUTER _____   Always Sometimes Rarely

How it helps me be successful: _____

_____

How it gets in the way: _____

_____

X-BOX   _____   Always   Sometimes   Rarely
(OR OTHER VIDEO GAMES)
How it helps me be successful: _____

_____

How it gets in the way: _____

_____

iPOD   _____   Always Sometimes Rarely
(OR OTHER MP3)
How it helps me be successful: _____

_____

How it gets in the way: _____

_____

DIGITAL   _____   Always Sometimes Rarely
ASSISTANT (PDA)
How it helps me be successful: _____

_____

How it gets in the way: _____

_____

INTERNET   _____   Always Sometimes Rarely
How it helps me be successful: _____

_____

How it gets in the way: _____

_____

INSTANT
MESSENGER
_____   Always Sometimes Rarely

How it helps me be successful: _____
_____

How it gets in the way: _____
_____

EMAIL
_____   Always Sometimes Rarely

How it helps me be successful: _____
_____

How it gets in the way: _____
_____

OTHER
TECHNOLOGY
_____   Always Sometimes Rarely

How it helps me be successful: _____
_____

How it gets in the way: _____
_____

TOTAL HOURS: _____

As you review the hours you spend using technology, what conclusions do you draw? Does it impact you positively or negatively? Do you have a better life? Are you better positioned to be more successful? Compare how much time you spend overall with technology to the time you spend doing the other important things in your life, like going to class, eating meals, playing sports, or spending time with your friends and family. Is your use of technology positively impacting you or not?

Limit the time you spend on your cell phone.

Who doesn't love his or her cell phone? When your friend is going to be late meeting you, for instance, he or she conveniently texts or calls you. Your cell phone gives you unlimited access to the world around you. It helps you stay connected to those who matter to you, stay informed of last minute social events, and allows you to carry on conversations without actually talking via texting! These upsides, however, have a major downside; you are always connected. You are always accessible.

When you have a 20-page paper to write, for example, incoming calls and text messages are distractions. They are also more exciting than writing your research paper which is due in two days! If you are constantly *available*, as technology allows you to be, you are constantly *unavailable* to the tasks that require your focused attention. To stay focused when studying, keep your cell phone out of sight and out of mind.

You own your cell phone, it should not own you. Turn it off when you are in class, reading, having coffee in the student center with your new friends, watching a movie, or eating dinner. Pay attention to the tasks at hand or people in front of you! Be present. You turn *on* the possibilities when you turn your cell phone *off*.

Schedule phone calls home.

Your cell phone makes it easy and convenient to call or text home whenever you want; on the spur of the moment and often. Be careful, however, calling home frequently can negatively impact your personal growth and development.

For example, if you receive a notice from the financial aid office telling you of a problem with your account on campus, don't immediately call your mom. Stop and think first. College is about becoming increasingly independent − solving your *own* problems, creating your *own* relationships, and taking responsibility for your *own* life. Instead of panicking, walk over to the financial aid office and try to solve your problem. If you do call home for your nightly conversation, you'll be able to demonstrate your growing maturity by sharing how you solved your own dilemma!

This doesn't mean don't call home, but you do need to limit the time you spend involving your parents, family, and friends in solving your problems. The only way you will become more independent is to literally speak less often with the "security blankets" in your life and rely more on your own decision making skills and reasoning. Learn how to deal with disappointment, frustration and situations your peers are also trying to handle. To avoid the "reactionary" call home, identify a consistent time once, or twice, a week to reach out and have a conversation with loved ones.

Treat yourself to technology down time.

Where do you go to escape the pressure, noise and distraction of constant accessibility and communication? Remove yourself from the never ending stimulus in your world by getting into a book or magazine. Let your mind be taken to a completely different place, someone else's world and imagination. You can do a Sudoku or crossword puzzle, browse through a magazine, or read the daily newspaper. Discover the "old fashioned" way of calming down by engaging in a technology-free internal dialogue. Along the way, you will re-discover your own imagination.

Have face to face conversations before jumping on Facebook.

Social networking allows you to share connections with people of similar interests, thoughts and feelings from all over the world.

Funny how these same people are right on campus with you or down the hall. You might miss the opportunity to meet face-to-face with them because you are on Facebook! Try to have real conversations in college instead of virtual ones!

Messaging someone on Facebook is easier than walking up to a new classmate and starting a conversation. Why not risk meeting amazing people? You can enjoy both types of relationships, yet having real conversations will allow you to network, find study partners, and practice speaking to strangers. Being able to meet people is a valuable skill. The more you practice, the easier it will become.

GET INVOLVED IN STUDENT ORGANIZATIONS.

Don't get trapped into thinking the only thing to do on campus when you aren't in class is to look at a screen of some type. One of the greatest benefits of your tuition dollars is the assortment of student activities and involvements at your disposal. By getting involved in a group, club, intramural sport, organization, or residence hall council committee, you can broaden your horizons and begin to expand your life experiences.

Numerous diverse student organizations exist on college campuses, including the yoga club, Engineers Without Borders, and Asian student union. There are dozens of activities you can explore. Find one that sparks your interest or simply sounds like fun, then consider attending their events or joining. In almost all cases, there is no fee!

How do you get involved? At the beginning of the school year, there will be an activities fair or postings of the student clubs and organizations available to you. Go to your school's website and you can not only find a listing of all the diverse ways to get connected, but you will usually find a calendar of events. Don't be shy! You don't need an invitation to attend; just show up and let someone there know you are possibly interested in joining. You can also visit your student activities or involvement office to learn how to contribute to your campus community.

ATTEND CAMPUS EVENTS.

Put that joystick down! Get out of your room or apartment! It's time to check out the fun taking place on campus paid for by your student activity fee. Stop by an activity sponsored by a club whose mission interests you. If you're into politics check out this month's lecture by the Young Democrats or Young Republicans; you might hear a great speaker or meet like-minded folks with whom you can connect and befriend. In addition, campus events are great opportunities to invite classmates to do something with you outside of class. They give you a break from your routine and can be intellectually stimulating.

Most events don't cost anything and are held on campus. There are also events held off-campus, especially those with community service components. It's a great idea to take advantage of opportunities to get away for a bit. The programming board is in charge of spending a large percentage of your activity fee. This is a great organization filled with positive students seeking creative ways to enhance campus life. They have committees ranging from Fine Arts, Lectures and Recreation to Publicity. You can learn skills of organization, planning and teamwork. Programming boards are always looking for members!

TAKE ADVANTAGE OF CAMPUS FACILITIES.

What makes up your college experience? Besides sitting in your room, eating in the campus center or working in the computer lab, how else could you interface with your surroundings?

The student center or student union is a comfortable place to grab a coffee, shop, do some reading, and find out what's happening on campus. Considered the "living room" or "heart beat" of campus, the student center is a hub of energy and activity, the perfect place to recharge your battery (and not only the one in your laptop!)

The library on a college campus is not like your public library at home. It's a great place to jump start your thinking and concentration. When you need to study quietly or get academic work done in a short amount of time, free from distraction, go to the library. There are study rooms where you can connect with your classmates. Rather than exchanging edits to your group presentation via email, you can reserve the media room and discuss edits as a group.

If you are seeking a spiritual life, check out campus ministry or a religiously-based student organization. Regardless of your religion, most universities offer places for personal reflection, and staff members to facilitate conversations around faith and religion.

Recreation facilities no longer consist of free weights and a few aerobic classes. Odds are your campus has a state-of-the-art fitness center resembling the most modern health club! Included in your tuition, you have access to exercise equipment, running machines, mats, weights, and classes ranging from spinning to yoga. Many include a pool, track, squash courts and climbing walls. Getting into the habit of "going to the gym" is not only good for you in the long run, it's a great place to make social connections while staying fit.

Did You Know?

"University" is a shortening of the Latin *universitas magistrorum et scholarium* or "a community of masters and scholars."

[Source: *www.facts.randomhistory.com*]

"Great minds discuss ideas;
average minds discuss events;
small minds discuss people."

- Eleanor Roosevelt

Random Thoughts...

Chapter 12

NOW FACTOR SIX

WHEN YOU TAKE CARE OF TODAY TOMORROW HAPPENS

"Most of us plateau when we lose the tension between where we are and where we ought to be."

John Gardner

LIVE IN THE PRESENT.

Worry about today. When you take it one day at a time, you will be less stressed and more productive. Don't cause yourself undue pressure by "cutting off your nose to spite your face." You'll look silly and still be frazzled. In other words, start replacing unproductive behaviors and attitudes with helpful ones. For example, maybe you were never one to be described as "tidy," but starting today, you can make a decision to "clean up" your act – literally! Decide to decide.

Can you go from "sloppy" to "tidy?" Getting where you want begins with knowing where you are! Why clean up if you don't consider yourself messy? Why study if you consider yourself a good student now? Living in the present requires a daily assessment (or inventory) to "keep it real." You benefit by knowing your "point of departure" because it suggests just how far you need to go and the work involved.

Another reason to pay immediate attention to your surroundings is because growth and knowledge acquisition are cumulative. What you learn, for example, builds upon what you already know. Don't miss the opportunities around you. Live in the present by being present! After all, when you take care of today, tomorrow works out just fine.

DEVELOP EFFECTIVE ORGANIZATIONAL SKILLS.

To be *organized* is to have your environment support your goals. It is when the spending of your time is consistent with your priorities. Effective organizational skills allow you to have immediate access to information and resources, approach situations prepared, and study efficiently. You will also handle the unknown with grace and greater ease, concentrate better and be able to adjust when thrown a curve ball or two.

Taking care of today doesn't mean forgetting about tomorrow or looming deadlines. It means giving yourself planning time, effective organizational structure or routines, and using the tools at your disposal on a daily basis. It means chipping away at tasks until they are completed and taking advantage of the smaller units of time which eventually add up.

Many students make the mistake of waiting until they have a chunk of time to read chapters or start a project. College doesn't come with large units of free time; it comes with an hour here and there. You have to schedule the big chunks of time, while taking advantage of the smaller segments that come between classes, before dinner, and after work. Use any time you have as productive time.

THINKING PAD

Question to Ask: What are my greatest challenges around organization?

_____
_____
_____
_____
_____
_____
_____
_____
_____

One of the best ways to be organized is to establish systems and routines, use proper storage containers and pay attention to the management of your paperwork. Search no more! There's no need to ruffle through stacks and stacks of papers on your desk (or under it) wasting valuable time and causing frustration. If you take an afternoon to really organize your paperwork and systems for handling your paperwork, you won't have to spend time looking for something you need, when you need it!

How to Manage Your Paperwork:

- Establish filing systems by category and date – "Reference Files."
- Keep files used most often in the front – "Active Files."
- Keep access numbers and PIN numbers in a folder and mail a copy to someone you trust.
- Take a photo copy of all of your credit cards.
- Handle a piece of mail only once – open it over a trash can.
- Read all of your mail when you get it.
- After paying a bill, immediately file it.
- Circle deadlines on paperwork; place in priority order.

USE A DAILY PLANNER.

To avoid the post-college nightmare of walking into class ready to take your final exam and being told it was yesterday, use a daily planner! One of the greatest tools you will use during your college years and beyond is a planner. This tool offers the ability to quickly review your daily schedule, update or edit obligations, deadlines and test dates, and quickly determine if you can "afford" to stray from your schedule. The planner gives you the ability to glance at the entire week or month. You can (and should) carry this tool around with you to class, meetings and work.

There are hard copy styles of daily planners like the Covey Daily Planner systems or the electronic kinds found in Blackberries or Palm Pilots. Use your planner to create routines in your schedule like "morning run," "breakfast," "laundry and study time," and "planning time." Yes… you need to plan on planning time! You should get in the habit of looking at your planner every morning and updating it throughout the day. At the end of the day, take a look at what you have in store for tomorrow. Move any items you didn't get done to the next day.

To help reinforce the positive outcomes of a planner use "Post It" notes around your environment, especially on your mirror or computer screen. This practice helps to remind you of the "must dos" and helps you avoid the negative consequences of forgetting to pay bills, hand in assignments, change the oil in your car, and so on!

LEARN TO SAY, "NO."

Learning to say, "No" is learning how to say, "I have other priorities right now." It's the ability to say, "I like to have fun as much as the next guy, but I have made a commitment to my academics or leadership position or family, and need to study." When you learn to say, "Not today," you are also saying, "I am in control." You can't spend time you don't have!

Saying, "Maybe later" is not saying, "No." Be honest in your communications. If you don't have time, or just don't want to do something, express yourself clearly. Avoid sending mixed messages. Otherwise, you are only delaying saying, "No" while annoying those who thought you'd be available "later."

Another habit that will serve you well is to say, "No" to over sleeping and get up a half hour earlier so you can eat a healthy breakfast. This is not an activity you can put off until tomorrow. You can't delegate your energy management to someone else. But, you can delete some things or ask for help when you need it. Make room for those people to whom you want to say, "Yes!"

Thinking Pad

Question to Ask: If I had two extra hours a day, what would I do with it?

_____

_____

_____

_____

_____

_____

_____

Remove temptations or distractions.

Who controls your world? Most of the time... you do! Why does it feel you are *being managed* instead of *managing* your life? Take control by eliminating those things (and people) which allow you to put off what needs to be done today. The first step is to identify the various and creative ways you are tempted and distracted! Do any of the following sound too familiar?

Sources of Distraction:

- Looking out the window
- Checking your email
- Tweeting
- Looking up obscure facts on the Internet
- Dozing off
- Singing along to the music
- Turning pages without comprehending what you're reading
- Doodling on your notes
- Talking to friends who interrupt you
- Taking phone calls

- Calling or texting friends
- Noticing your nails need to be done
- Painting your nails
- Wondering if the Mac and Cheese from last night is still edible
- Thoughts of being elsewhere
- Worrying about everything you have to get done
- Missing your dog from home (even if you never had a dog)
- Wondering what you'd look like with a different hair color

How can you be less distracted and more focused on the tasks at hand? First, anticipate what distracts you, then control it. You can spend two hours reading a thirty page chapter because your mind keeps wandering or you are constantly interrupted, or you can put into practice some of the methods below and be efficient in your concentration efforts! Work smarter not harder!

METHODS FOR REDUCING DISTRACTIONS:

- Set times your cell phone is turned on. Turn it off during study time.
- Leave electronics locked in your desk during the day.
- Don't be on the internet while doing work.
- Remove yourself from high traffic areas when you need to concentrate.
- Find a specific place to study and get work done, away from your dorm room.
- Let friends know when you are "available" to socialize.
- Enlist the support of someone to keep you on task.
- Give yourself a "deadline" for achieving a goal.
- Plan to arrive 15 minutes early to your commitments and appointments.
- Do not listen to loud music or songs with lyrics while studying.
- Close your room door.

THINK BIG PICTURE.

The beginning of every week is a prime opportunity to get a "feel" for the week ahead. Think big picture by considering how every action has a consequence. What are the more stressful things you have to get done, the fun things and those which won't take much time? What are you looking forward to, and what is going to be a challenge? Not only does this assist in the management of your energy, but it mentally softens the blow! You get to emotionally prepare yourself for the good, bad, joyful and challenging.

You can prevent your greatest challenges from "getting away from you" by tackling them first. This is called the "Frogs First" approach. In the same way frogs can literally "jump away" from you, so can those things you really don't want to do. When you do these least favorite tasks first, you get them done. It's all downhill from there.

Examples of doing "Frogs First" is to do the homework for your least favorite subject first, pay your bills on Saturday morning before you go for a walk, or workout before you go shopping! Do that which you most don't want to do first!

Obvious (but never overstated) suggestions for stepping back from the details long enough to access the bigger picture include the following:

- Reward yourself for getting through something challenging.
- Be willing to let go of time consuming commitments with little satisfaction.
- Ask for help when you need it.
- Go to study skills sessions whether you think you need them or not.
- Be proactive in preparing for major projects or events.

- Work backward to establish a time line for use in your planner.
- Break down large projects and assignments into smaller ones using deadlines.

ATTEND TO YOUR SPACE AND PSYCHE.

What in your immediate environment inspires you to get productive? Is there more around you that encourages distractions and laziness or have you created physical and mental spaces where college success is encouraged?

Less is often more. Tidy beats out sloppiness. Clean outweighs dirty. Organized is better than chaotic. Control is better than freaking out. Now is the time to learn and implement valuable success strategies that will benefit you for the rest of your life! When your immediate environment is in order, you are confirming the reality that taking care of today sets up a good tomorrow. Order is perceived when your bed is made, your room is clean, you know where things are and you're not surrounded by clutter, or stacks of old pizza boxes.

ESSENTIAL TOOLS AND PRACTICES OF CONTROL:

- Throw out any clothes in your closet and drawers you haven't worn in a year.
- Invest in stackable storage and filing units, then label them.
- Use your closet space creatively.
- Invest in a wall calendar to record "big picture" events and appointments.
- Surround yourself with inspirational sayings or visuals.
- Avoid or remove "clutter" – less gives you a feeling of being under control.
- Ask questions until you know what is expected of you.

- Learn to recognize peer pressure and stay true to your priorities.
- Find people with similar values to befriend.
- Attend leadership training workshops.
- Pick up before going to bed every night.
- Do your laundry on a consistent basis – don't save it up…

There is great freedom in taking care of today. Although you can't control what the day might bring, you can control how you respond. Class is scheduled when it is scheduled. There are seven (not eight) days in a week. Final exams are during Final Exam week. The rest of the time, however, is yours to manage. Figure out how to manage your time by answering the kinds of questions below:

- How do I want my physical space to support my goals?
- What strategies of organization are important to my success?
- How am I going to ensure a limitation of interruptions while I am studying?
- What specific tools of organization do I need to purchase and put into practice?
- How are my current organizational skills serving me?
- What segments of time do I need to block out on a weekly basis and for what activity?
- What are the activities I tend to delay?
- Where do I get the most accomplished?
- Why is there value in changing current energy management behaviors?
- The most important tasks to include in every school day include what?
- The overview of the week needs to take place when and how?
- What currently consumes the biggest blocks of my day?
- How effective is the time allocated to personal health and wellness?

- The desired outcome of better organization and management of energy is what?

THINKING PAD

Question to Ask: What will be the "rules" of my college career? How do I want to play what isn't a game at all?

_____
_____
_____
_____
_____
_____
_____
_____

FIND WAYS TO KEEP YOURSELF MOTIVATED.

How do you give yourself a needed kick in the butt? There are many things you can do to add a skip to your step or motivate yourself to keep doing what needs to be done. The more you focus on being a productive college student, the more motivational strategies you will need to use.

WAYS TO GET MOTIVATED:

- Remember! Change only happens when you act!
- Break down tasks into manageable pieces.
- Do something – anything.
- Start small. Build.
- Stay focused. Simplify.
- Dress up for class.
- Let go of people, places and things that bring you down or block your efforts.

- Take the time to consider your priorities.
- Care about your emotional, spiritual, physical and intellectual health.
- Surround yourself with positive people.
- Find a role model or mentor.
- Read inspirational books.
- Connect your readership to your leadership.
- Eat breakfast every morning.
- Take a walk every day.
- Stop to watch others you admire. What do you really see?
- Don't major in the minors.
- Reward yourself for small accomplishments.
- Talk to a counselor.
- Make a daily TO DO list.
- Talk about your goals with friends and strangers.
- Ask for help when you need it.
- Spend time alone to contemplate.
- Associate with people who are doing what you want to do.
- Be willing to pay your dues.
- Praise yourself out loud. Never speak negatively of others.
- Get a "thinking" chair.
- Smile more. Laugh more. Look around more.
- Attend motivational seminars.
- Volunteer. It teaches you to count your blessings.

RUN (DON'T WALK) AWAY FROM PROCRASTINATION.

What causes millions of college students to jeopardize a good grade and lie to their professors most often? What is the number one stumbling block that trips up new students? Procrastination. Defined as the practice of postponing priorities, *procrastination* will undoubtedly interfere with your potential academic achievement and success. William J. Knaus, cognitive psychologist and author of the book, *Do It Now! Break the Procrastination* estimates approximately 90% of college students procrastinate and of these college students who submit to procrastination, 25% are chronic procrastinators. These procrastinators often drop or withdraw from college courses, or worse: they eventually end up failing out and/or dropping out of college.

REASONS BEHIND PROCRASTINATION:

- Negative internal dialogue regarding the task
- Poor time management
- Poor concentration (can't focus)
- The task is boring
- Perfectionism
- The task is overwhelming
- Don't know where to begin
- Don't know how to begin
- Fear of Failure
- Fear of Success
- Fear of Rejection
- Fear of the Unknown

The process of understanding why you and others procrastinate is a critical step toward conquering and defeating this destructive habit. To overcome and conquer your tendency to put off the inevitable, ask yourself the following questions:

- Who? Who do you find yourself procrastinating around? Is it everyone or is it just a certain professor, instructor, boyfriend, or girlfriend?
- What and how? What activities take the place of your school assignments? How are you spending your time when you procrastinate? Notice patterns. Are you people-watching at the library or do you choose to do the dishes and clean your

room instead of doing your work? Do you habitually turn on the TV?

- When? Are you likely to procrastinate in the morning or in the evening (or both times)? What times of the day are you most likely to disengage from your homework and school assignments? When are you at your best and most focused on the task at hand?
- Where? Where are you likely to procrastinate? In your room, sitting in the library, or after working out in the fitness center?
- Why? What's the motivation behind your procrastination? Is the task too big? Are you having trouble getting started? Are you having trouble figuring out the rules of the task?

Everyone procrastinates from time to time. Your goal as a college student is to make sure that procrastination does not steal your dreams, goals and aspirations. Believe it or not, there are college students who never procrastinate and get their schoolwork done on time, if not earlier. These are the students who are tipping the grading curve in their desired direction and achieving their goals. Procrastinators, on the other hand, are always struggling to get their work in on time and rarely cross items off of their TO DO lists.

Stay away from starting a project until the night before it is due. Discover the times when you are most productive as a college student and effectively make use of that time. Pretend everything is due right away and get your school assignments done as soon as possible! It is also helpful to use homework assignments that give you enjoyment or bring a great sense of achievement, as a reward. This practice will help give you the fuel you need to approach homework assignments you deem boring and draining.

Always remember that billions of dreams, goals and aspirations have gone unfulfilled as a result of putting off what needs to be done sooner not later. Recognize when you begin to sabotage your success with procrastination and give yourself a kick in the butt!

Did You Know?

Alexander Lucius Twilight was the first African American to graduate with a four year college degree from Middlebury College in 1823.

[Source: www.wikipedia.org]

"If a man insisted always on being serious, and never allowed himself a bit of fun and relaxation, he would go mad – or become unstable without knowing it."

- Herodotus

Random Thoughts...

Chapter 13

NOW FACTOR SEVEN

BEING UNDECLARED IS NOT NECESSARILY BEING UNDECIDED

"College students should embrace life by chasing adventures and laughing at their mistakes while having the courage to face fears and the confidence to succeed in everything. Sure, there will be challenges along the way, but it is these moments that they will most remember and reflect on in life."

Julie R. Beck, World Traveler
Mount Olive, North Carolina

Try taking a Pass/Fail course.

Wouldn't it be intimidating to be told at new student orientation you had to know what you were doing for the rest of your life? What if you were also told you couldn't change your mind? Pretty scary and stressful if these were true statements. Despite what some mischievous upperclassmen may tell you, there is plenty of time to figure it all out.

Going to college doesn't mean you know what you want in life, let alone what to study or what major to pursue. Making a decision on a major, for example, is a process like buying a car. You can "test drive" a few models before you actually buy one. All sorts of factors, such as personal interests, academic strengths, and classroom experiences, impact your feelings towards a particular major. Taking a course pass/fail is a good way to see whether or not you get excited about that particular subject. There is no penalty because there is no grade assigned, only a "P" for pass or an "F" for fail.

Take the first few years to explore your options. Ask faculty members and other students about specific classes and majors. Eventually, you will feel confident in your decision. Reach out and seek out people who can help you make an informed decision such as peer mentors, academic advisors, or career services specialists. In the end, the choice is yours to make.

Look for the Telling Signs.

The famous philosopher Heraclitus said, "Nothing endures but change." Through your course of study, you may want to change it up a few times. It's better to alter your direction now then confirm *after* you graduate how much you dislike the topic or field! It's also OK to enter college not knowing what career you want to pursue. Test the waters. Change majors. Go undeclared.

How do you know a major isn't for you? If you lack interest in what the professors are saying during most of your classes, find it hard to get into active discussions about subjects in your major, or struggle to receive decent grades in required courses, consider the possibility you're in the wrong major. Ask yourself, "Am I excited about what I am learning?" You can also ask questions and seek guidance from your academic advisor, or department chairperson.

Sometimes it's helpful to re-evaluate the following:

- *Why did I come to college?*

  _____
  _____
  _____
  _____

- *What am I good at?*

  _____
  _____
  _____

- *What subjects are coming easily to me?*

  _____
  _____
  _____
  _____

- *What do I hope to achieve at the end of college?*

  _____
  _____
  _____
  _____

- *What classes do I like most?*

  _____

  _____

  _____

  _____

- *Who can help me find out more information about a major?*

  _____

These questions will help you prepare for important conversations about your choice of major.

STAY IN TOUCH WITH YOUR ACADEMIC ADVISOR.

Are you a person who seeks out help when you are struggling or waits for help to come to you? Academic advisors help students organize and plan their course of study. They are considered "the academic experts" of the college or university, and can be thought of as the equivalent of a high school guidance counselor. However in most cases, they are a faculty member in your major. In college, you are responsible for initiating contact with your academic advisor. They will not seek you out.

It is important to make a connection with your academic advisor the first few weeks of each semester. Don't miss out on all of the opportunities and valuable guidance they can offer during your college career. Academic advisors are also the first people you can turn to for a job recommendation – but they can't help you if they don't know you! Since academic advisors are busy with their own schedules, making an appointment or dropping by during office hours is the best way to ensure a meeting. Hint! Faculty members enjoy conversations over coffee or lunch. Be pro-active and seek them out.

For example, when you receive a bad grade on an exam or

paper, don't know what courses to take next semester, want to study abroad, have issues with a particular professor, or seek career advice, touch base with your academic advisor. Be open to learning from him or her. Creating a positive relationship begins with you. If for some reason you don't connect, request a different advisor by seeing the dean of the department.

TIPS ON A SUCCESSFUL RELATIONSHIP WITH YOUR ACADEMIC ADVISOR:

- Set-up an initial meeting to introduce yourself.
- Plan out your major course of study.
- Seek their help when struggling with your courses.
- Be on time and show up for every meeting.
- Say thank you for their help.
- Listen to what they have to say.
- Ask questions.
- Be prepared with questions.
- Take notes.
- Be honest.
- Keep a positive attitude.
- Be pro-active, not reactive.
- Ask about expectations and responsibilities.
- Touch base with advisor more than two times a year.

"Reading makes a full man,
conference a ready man,
and writing an exact man."

- Sir Francis Bacon

Random Thoughts...

Chapter 14

NOW FACTOR EIGHT

YOU WILL GET HIGHER GRADES BY SITTING IN THE FRONT ROW

"Yes, you may have the gift of prophecy, you may
have the gift of scientific prediction and understand
the behavior of molecules, you may break into the
storehouse of nature and bring forth many new insights:
yes, you may ascend to the heights of academic
achievement so that you have all knowledge and you
may boast of your great institutions of learning and the
boundless extent of your degrees; but if you have not
love, all of these mean absolutely nothing."

Dr. Martin Luther King, Jr.

SIT IN THE FRONT ROW OF CLASS.

Where do you find yourself most comfortable in a classroom? Do you arrive early to class and seek the front row, or are you five minutes late and sneak in the back where no one can see you? Do you think the front row is reserved for only the really smart students?

The front row *is* where "smart" students sit! They demonstrate their interest in learning and are ready to engage in the most effective ways. As students you get rewarded for your good work and performance. Sitting in front makes you more attentive, inspires you to answer questions, and usually results in a higher grade than sitting in the back of the room. Being closer to the professor also means you will hear his or her words better. It's not as easy to "tune out" or "dose off" in the front because people are watching you. As a student you have a choice, to sit in the front and be considered one of the "smart kids" or sit in the back and "dose off." It sounds like being in the front row may not be so bad after all!

LEARN HOW TO LEARN.

As a baby, you learned how to walk. As a toddler, you learned how to talk. As a child, you learned how to write or ride a bike. As a teenager, you learned how to drive. All of these things required someone teaching or showing you how to do them. You required guidance (or instruction) until you mastered each new skill. In other words, you *learned* how to learn.

With every unfamiliar experience, you will need to adjust. You come to college with a certain skill set and wonder why what you have been used to doesn't work anymore. Each professor has a different syllabus, a different grading policy, and a different teaching style. Because of this, college students often need to "learn how to learn" again. Expectations suddenly change. You learn inside of the classroom, but the most important thing is what you do outside of the classroom to better that learning. You may discover your philosophy professor, for instance, wants a different style of writing than your history professor. Make the necessary adjustments!

Taking advantage of study skills sessions, including discovering your learning style and how you should study for certain courses, will improve your ability to learn. Such resources are found at the academic resource center. Learning how to become a better time manager and planning out your "study time" are essential competencies for success. Grab your friends and make time for a campus tour to locate the academic advising, or academic resources offices, on campus!

READ THE ADDITIONAL READING LIST.

Imagine it's the first day of a new class. You skim the syllabus focusing on what books are under the "required" section and need to be purchased. Somehow, without even knowing, you skip over the "suggested" readings and move right onto course objectives and grading policies. You fail to pay attention to the significant details and recommended readings because you falsely believe "not required" means "not important." Guess again!

Suggested (or additional) readings offer additional information to help you better understand the required material and teach you something you didn't already know about the subject area. Professors add suggested readings to the syllabus or course for a reason, and it's not to fill an empty space on the page. It's all fair game for a professor to assume you've read this material and include it on a test, or expect to see it referenced in a paper you are required to write.

Before you don't read the additional reading list, ask yourself, "But what if I do get tested on it? Who can I blame?" Wouldn't it be better to be more prepared and knowledgeable? Wouldn't it be better to take the extra steps and manage your time appropriately so you can fit in your reading – all of it? This will increase your ability to get an "A" in the class! Taking that extra step will get you there! So next time you see the word "suggested;" consider it required!

PARTICIPATE IN CLASSROOM DISCUSSIONS.

Are you attentive in class? What if your professor calls on you to share your thoughts but you dosed off and can't even remember her question? Most likely, you would find your face turning red as the professor reminds your entire class that 20% of the course grade comes from participation in classroom discussions. To make a bad situation worse, the friend on your right is laughing because they are so relieved he or she wasn't caught day-dreaming.

Engaging in classroom discussion helps you clarify any questions you may have on a particular topic, and allows you to contribute to a conversation. Class participation shows you care about the class and what is being discussed. Sometimes classes are so large that without participating in classroom discussion, your professor may never get to know you. Backing up your opinions in a classroom is also great preparation for a diversity of workplace situations. You will learn how to confidently make an argument and apply critical thinking. The best benefit of participation in class is that it's the easiest 10% or 20% of a good grade to earn. All you have to do is speak up!

ASK QUESTIONS WHEN YOU DON'T UNDERSTAND.

Did you ever get scared to ask a question because you were afraid it would be considered "dumb" or have an obvious answer?

Did you ever think to yourself, "It's better not to ask, I'll just figure it out later on my own!" but then never went back to figure it out later and still had the same question? No question is a bad one, with one exception. Never let yourself ask, "Professor, are you going to be doing anything important in class today?"

Being a successful student means recognizing that it's good to ask questions. The moment you have a question, and don't ask, is the moment you increase the likelihood of not knowing the answer on a test. No one gets punished for asking a question, but students do punish themselves by not asking. Most likely, many other students in the class have the same question, but are just as afraid to ask. Take the time to send an email to your professor after class, visit his or her office hours, or speak with them after class. Understanding what you are taught is your responsibility. Ignoring what you don't know is a bad strategy.

To a professor, asking a question is a good thing. It shows you care about the course, but more importantly, you care about your learning!

PAY THE COST TO BE THE BOSS.

How much does your dream cost? How much will it cost you to achieve your academic dream? All dreams, goals, and aspirations have a price tag attached to them which must be honored – just not with money. The currency is mental, emotional and physical sacrifices. The million dollar question is: Are you ready and willing to pay the cost to graduate with a college degree?

As a college student, you must accept the fact that just because you register for a course and perform minimum work doesn't give you a passport to an above average passing grade. Just showing up isn't sufficient enough to succeed in college. There are no easy roads to college success. Registering for a college course is easy, pursuing your academic goals will require effort, energy, enthusiasm and commitment.

What do you have to "pay?" Consider which of the following you may have to "spend" in exchange for academic success. You will quickly discover, in order to get good grades and understand what you are learning, you will have to give (or give up) a few things!

POTENTIAL AND REALISTIC ACADEMIC CHOICES:

- Going to your study group meeting instead of watching your favorite episode of The Deadliest Catch
- Putting your Facebook status on "hold" during the two weeks prior to finals
- Getting up an hour earlier to workout and relieve the stress associated with too much to do
- Hurting your friend's feelings by not always being available to socialize because you need to finish your paper
- Not returning the gazillion text messages you get every evening because you don't bring your phone to the library with you

Chapter 15

NOW FACTOR NINE

ABSENCE MAKES YOUR GRADES GO DOWN

"One is not born into the world to do everything, but to do something."

Henry David Thoreau

Go to class.

Before iPods, Wii, iPads and the internet, there was a time when soap operas were all the rage on college campuses. At 3 p.m. on any given day, students (men and women alike) were tuned into General Hospital to see what would be next for Luke and Laura. Because the technology to Tivo "GH" hadn't been invented, students would choose to skip class, show up late or attend with a poor attitude. Missing GH took great discipline! Times have changed. Luke and Laura who?

When your professor tells you, "I understand there will be times when you won't be able to make it to class," he or she is not implying you can miss class or be late for silly reasons. The following list of "thin," "light," "weak," or "lame" reasons to skip class (or show up late) are *not* legitimate. Honesty is a good practice and should be used when you have a legitimate reason for not being in class.

The Non-Legit Excuses for Skipping Class or Being Late:

- I can get the information from the text book.
- The lecture is disorganized and boring.
- I can get notes from my friends.
- I am too tired.
- The professor doesn't take attendance.

Pick class times to optimize your learning.

Are you a morning bird or a night owl? The most meaningful and productive work gets done between the hours of 5 a.m. and 10 a.m. Is this your natural "primetime?" If so, select classes in the morning when you are given the option. Early morning classes can be tough to handle if you are (or become) a late night talker who socializes until 1 a.m. and then starts your homework. You will need to schedule your courses mid-morning or in the afternoon.

Although "college time" is different than the rest of the world, having knowledge of your body rhythms, brain drain hours, desired activities, and wellness habits should drive your schedule making. When this isn't possible, you will have to make the necessary adjustments. Most likely, something will have to give!

For example, if you have morning classes and are a night owl, you will need to have lights out at a reasonable hour affording you no less than six to eight hours of sleep a night. Your routine will have to change, if only for one semester. When you have evening classes, you will have to find ways of staying alert, attentive and participatory during class! Sleeping in class is not an option.

GOOD WAYS TO STAY AWAKE IN CLASS:

- Eat a nutritious and light meal before class.
- Go for a run or brisk walk one hour before class.
- Take a shower.
- Put on nice clothes.
- Grab a cold bottle of water to drink on your way.
- Listen to upbeat music on your way to class.
- Meet up with a classmate a half hour before class for refreshments.
- Sit in the front row.

BAD WAYS TO STAY AWAKE IN CLASS:

- Drink three Redbulls on your way.
- Eat a heavy meal.
- Not give yourself enough time to get there.
- Be hung over.
- Rely on stimulants.

Honor your professor.

You will receive the respect you earn. Your professors, however, need to be respected from the very start given their level of expertise, preparation and dedication to advancing your intellect. You can demonstrate this respect by taking responsibility for your learning, exercising self-discipline, handing in assignments of high quality, being prepared for class, participating in discussions and dressing in a manner reflective of your love of learning. You will feel a sense of pride, and most likely end up with a better grade!

Take advantage of opportunities to be an active participate in your learning by avoiding disrespectful behaviors such as:

- Answering questions with, "I didn't read the assignment for today"
- Never maintaining eye contact with your professor
- Showing up late
- Talking during class while the professor is teaching
- Doing less than you are capable of doing
- Sleeping in class
- Not asking questions when you don't understand
- Chewing and popping gum during class
- Sitting in the back row

Introduce yourself to your classmates.

Not only is your professor deserving of respect, so are your classmates. You can show them respect and honor by introducing yourself to those you sit near. Do the grown-up thing by extending your hand and saying, "Hello. My name is…" The worst outcome is you get ignored. The best outcome is you get greeted kindly before every class!

Once you have been introduced, it is polite and respectful to use someone's name every time you are in their presence. It's not easy to remember names, is it? You might be among those who forget names as they are being shared!

How to Remember Names of Classmates:

- When you first hear it, repeat it in a sentence
- After getting someone's name, go write it down in your class notebook
- Use their name three times during your greeting
- Replay the conversation in your mind and say the other person's name out loud
- Write a room chart and fill in every name (check it before class)
- Connect the name to something they say about themselves
- When you see them out of class, greet them again
- If you forget, tell them you've forgotten

CALCULATE THE ACTUAL DOLLAR VALUE OF A CLASS.

Do the math. When you skip one class of a fifteen week semester where you are carrying 15 credits, each one hour of missed class time represents one-fifteenth of fifty percent of your annual tuition. If you are paying $30,000 in tuition per year, that's $15,000 per semester. Based on taking five 3-credit courses (which totals 15 hours of class time per week) you are spending $3,000.00 for each ten week course or a total of $1,500.00 per week. If you are required to be in 15 hours of class per week, that's rather easy math. Every one hour of class you skip is costing you $100.00! If your college tuition is "only" $15,000.00 per year, that's still $50.00 an hour for a skipped class. These figures do not include room and board.

Would you pay for a car and not drive it off the lot? Would

you order a pizza and after paying, not eat it? Then, why would you pay for an education and not get one? When you don't go to class, you are throwing money away!

This principle also applies to when your professor cancels class! Is that really OK with you? Are you getting the day off or not getting your money's worth? In college you can ask the professor in a kind way if a class will be made up, providing *you* aren't skipping any either. If you become concerned about the unlikely event your professor cancels more classes then he or she makes, it is most appropriate to talk to the dean of your department.

THINKING PAD

Question to Ask: Why is it hard to think of missing class in terms of throwing money away?

RESPECT THE RATIONALE FOR ATTENDANCE.

Ah, the age old question: If you do well on all exams, but have poor class attendance, should you be penalized? From a technical perspective, go by what is outlined in your course syllabus or student handbook. From an educational perspective, the rational for being in class is to contribute to class discussion, grow from the interactions between professor and student, and benefit from being part of a scholarly exchange. If you aren't there, you miss out on what it truly means to be part of an academic community!

To actively engage in your education means to be active in class. Whether you ask questions, answer questions, or sit in the front row and warmly greet your professor, you are making that class what it will be or not. Your presence matters. Likewise, if you go to class and distract from the process, or do absolutely nothing at all, you are also making that class what it will be or not. Make the learning experience productive, exciting, fun and intriguing! Give yourself credit for being more than a number on an exam; become a student with a name. That's how you learn!

Did You Know?

The most popular majors on a college campus according to the Princeton Review are Management/Business, Psychology, and Education.

"Seek not greatness, but seek truth and you find both."

- Horace Mann

Random Thoughts...

Chapter 16

NOW FACTOR TEN

TURNING PAGES ISN'T READING

"Success is doing what you enjoy doing and enjoying what you do."

Dr. Maureen Hartford, President
Meredith College, Raleigh, North Carolina

READ TO TEACH.

There is a difference between reading, studying and owning what you are reading. To *read* material is just that – to pass over words as if getting through a novel. When you take this surface approach, you're usually reading for fun – not comprehension, and fifty percent of what you read is lost after you have read it. This type of reading is not a good study technique.

To *study* material is to go over and over it until you take it from short term memory to long term memory where the material goes into the test with you. When you want to be able to recall information, you need to study it first.

The best approach to effective reading is to *own* what you read. This entails learning it well enough to teach it. You can make analogies and relate the material to other material you know. Owning your reading material is knowing the material cold, and understanding it so you can explain it to someone else. It's more than learning it long enough to regurgitate it for a test. This is how you should study!

How do you achieve this level of comprehension? Repetition. The more you "repeat" material, the more information you retain. For example, after you take chapter notes, go over them again and again. If you like acronyms, use them in your review process. Teach and quiz your study partners from what you've highlighted in your notes. Ask the same questions many times, yet in different ways. When you want to know if you've got it, give yourself a mini-test.

It will also help your reading comprehension to know when you are most effective in your studying habits. Are you a night time studier or a morning person? Knowing when you study best helps you waste less time as does knowing (then getting) the sleep you need. If you are always "running on empty," it will be harder to understand the material, even if it is your best time to study.

ALLOW ENOUGH TIME TO STUDY.

How much time do you need to spend studying? There are only 168 hours in a week. You need to eat, sleep, go to class, hang out with friends, and so on. So, how much of your time should you spend studying? More than you think!

Be deliberate, intentional and purposeful in regards to your study habits. Understand that, as a minimum, you will need to spend two hours studying for every hour you spend in class. This is a minimum and if you are studying to be a doctor or lawyer, that time can increase to four or five hours. Be practical about your time, make the best use of your time, and pace yourself. If you spend all your time on English because you like it but run out of time for Mathematics, you will fail mathematics and it won't really matter that you got an "A" in your English class. All your classes deserve your time and attention. It is helpful to plan out your day, including when you'll study and what you'll study. Then you can cross off the things you have accomplished and ride off of that success. Make sure you remember everything you need to do and make time for all of them.

FIND A QUIET PLACE TO READ.

Do you get distracted easily? If you are like the average college student that has multiple things going on at the same time, how could you not get distracted?

Taking time out of your day away from your residence hall, club or organization office, or the campus center, to focus on reading for your classes is crucial. Where do you go? The old fashioned library remains a quiet place for students to read. Find a quiet special spot or corner to "claim" as your own, and get in the habit of reading in the library. You'll get more done without distractions.

Aside from the library, a residence hall lounge, empty classroom, meeting room or even an off-campus site, may be just what you need to focus. Take the time to ask yourself, "Is where I'm reading or doing my homework a quiet and productive place?" If not, then it's time to move! Often a complete change of scenery (like a trip to Starbucks) improves concentration.

HIGHLIGHT THE IMPORTANT THINGS.

As a child in school you were introduced to this wonderful thing called a "highlighter." It seemed to make things "stand out" or appear more colorful. If you are a visual learner, you may have had color-coded sections, and may remember carrying multiple colors in your book bag. You might have highlighted everything in your text book you thought to be important. Next thing you knew, the whole chapter was highlighted. This may have looked nice, but it didn't help you.

Discovering what is important in a chapter is often difficult to decide, and it's often easier to highlight an entire paragraph so you don't miss the important stuff. Highlighting effectively is a learnable and necessary skill. It will save you time in the long run by reducing large content to what matters most. To highlight correctly, focus on important information such as dates, names, quotes, formulas, bolded or italic words, key terms, and sentences you would consider to be definitions. Trust your judgment. Your instincts will kick in.

Another helpful strategy for highlighting is to apply the five "Ws and How" approach you learned in grade school. Check your highlighted material after you finish reading. If you have highlighted the Who? What? Where? When? Why? and How? in that section, you've identified the "important stuff." You may also want to consider the question, "Do I need to know this?" If the answer is affirmative, then highlight it! Practice this technique on your next chapter reading!

SCHEDULE TIME TO RE-READ.

Quality and quantity go hand in hand. Reading a chapter once and never reading or reviewing it again increases your chances of not remembering the material at all! Wouldn't you consider it a waste of time to forget what you spent time to read? Repetition is what allows the information you learn to become part of your daily routine and knowledge. Remember when a coach told you practice makes perfect? By doing the same thing over and over again you got better at it.

Reading is the same way. Scheduling time every day to re-read a chapter section, gives you an opportunity to reflect on your reading. What you have reviewed makes better sense the second time around. The more you read, the more you get better at reading, and the more you understand a given topic. When you focus on increasing the *quantity* of your reading, you increase the *quality* of your comprehension. Isn't that the point?

TEST YOURSELF ON YOUR READING.

Just flipping those pages doesn't mean you actually know the information. You may have read a paper, but did you really read it? Have you ever walked away from reading an entire chapter only to ask yourself, "What did I just read?" Maybe you smiled and thought, "Yes, I'm done with 100 pages!" Ask yourself the tough question, "Do I understand what I just read?"

Skimming through a chapter, although a common college technique, takes away your ability to understand the material you are assigned. This "cutting corners" or "easy way out" strategy will not get you very far because it will create more work for you in the end. Right before exams, you will find yourself struggling to grasp what you skimmed. Consider using the much better option of reading and re-reading each chapter, then testing yourself for comprehension using a practice test you create.

Make a test by asking, "What question does each paragraph answer?" This becomes your study guide and ensures you fully understand what you read. To help formulate your chapter study guides, use the questions below.

What's the main question being answered in this paragraph?

_____

_____

_____

_____

_____

What questions do I still have about this chapter or section?

_____

_____

_____

_____

_____

What sample questions can I write to quiz myself on each paragraph?

_____

_____

_____

_____

_____

The knowledge gained from reading in college is meant to be cumulative. If you understand what you've read to the extent you can tell someone else about it, even teach him or her the content, you are ready to move onto your next assignment without looking back. If you don't, it means that you will have to re-visit it later. Bottom line, if you can't answer the above questions, you need to dedicate more time to your reading and strive for comprehension. If you can't explain it, you don't understand it.

"The most difficult thing is the decision to act, the rest is merely tenacity. The fears are paper tigers. You can do anything you decide to do. You can act to change and control your life; and the procedure, the process is its own reward."

- Amelia Earhart

Random Thoughts...

Chapter 17

NOW FACTOR ELEVEN

PROFESSORS ARE PEOPLE TOO

"Take a risk and step outside of your comfort zone; whether it be joining something new or meeting people different from you. College is a safe environment and now is the time!"

Shelby Harris, Director of Student Activities
University of Massachusetts, Boston

GET TO KNOW YOUR PROFESSORS.

Whether you take a psychology, math, physics or music course, every professor you encounter has something different to offer. Just like your teachers in high school brought a diversity of talents and experiences, your college professors will come from a variety of backgrounds and have fascinating life stories.

In college, you will connect with some professors more than others. You will find some professors more entertaining than others. There will be those professors who make you laugh, and those who make you cry. Take the time to get to know your professors. Professors are well educated and have chosen the path of empowering you to become a successful and impactful adult. Professors usually have Master's Degrees or PhD's. In some cases, they are leaders in their industry, have written books, short stories, and plays or have invented something you use on a daily basis. Some of your professors may have won national and international awards. All have inspired a new generation.

Take the time in every course to introduce yourself to your professor, and ask about their background, research and field of study. They will be excited to share this information with you. Don't be the student who ends each semester realizing not one of his or her professors knows anything about them – and vice versa!

GO TO OFFICE HOURS.

What are office hours? It's a time when you can "guarantee" your professor will be in his or her office. Use this time to ask questions, get extra help, or just stop by to say, "Hi." Universities and colleges require professors to have office hours and publish them. Write them down in your planner or online calendar. Make a point to attend at least one office hour for every professor during each semester or term. That will get you closer to creating a mutually beneficial relationship.

By attending office hours, you also send a message to your professors that you care about your education, and are willing to seek out extra help. Many freshmen seminar classes are huge making it difficult to ask questions during class or establish a rapport with the professor. Visiting your professor gives you an opportunity to be more than a number. You can also use office hours to review errors on papers, or discuss how to prepare for an upcoming exam. The only agenda is the one you set!

UNDERSTAND YOUR ROLE AS A STUDENT – NOT A CONSUMER.

Are you a "college student" or "consumer?" To better answer this question, consider the following scenario: Your professor puts material on a test you didn't realize you needed to know. You fail miserably. As a consumer, this feels very unfair, especially since you are paying tuition – which includes your professor's salary! However, as a student, you take responsibility for not being prepared, go back and check your notes only to discover you should have studied additional material! You take ownership for your learning versus feeling entitled to a degree.

College costs. Even though you pay a high price for your education, you remain a student no matter where you go, or how many dollars you pay. It is your responsibility to know what is expected of you on an exam, assignment, paper, and project. Same applies to knowing about college policies and procedures – especially your academic Code of Conduct. This is your end of the deal!

When you find yourself feeling entitled to a better grade because you are an "A" student who handed in a "C" paper, or you keep asking for deadline extensions because you were visiting friends, ask yourself, "Am I meeting my responsibilities as a 'college student,' or behaving as a 'consumer?'" Hopefully you will congratulate yourself for your maturity, or change your behaviors.

Chapter 18

NOW FACTOR TWELVE

CHEATING IS WHEN YOU DON'T DO YOUR OWN WORK

"Life is not divided into semesters. You don't get summers off and very few employers are interested in helping you find yourself."

Bill Gates

KNOW YOUR COLLEGE'S ACADEMIC POLICIES.

Take a moment once again to ask: What do I want most from my college experience?

To be successful?
To make great friends?
To receive good grades?
To get smarter?
To prepare for a successful career?
To choose the right profession?
To help others?
To learn how to learn?
To make mucho money after graduation?
All of the above?

To get any or all of these things involves one important component, *you* doing *your* best! When you fail to do your own work, study off of exam files in the fraternity house, or take a paper off of the internet, you are not doing your best. You are taking what isn't yours. This is a *violation* of all college and university academic Codes of Conduct.

Current research indicates today's college students prioritize serving their communities and making the world a better place. Stealing isn't in the mix and is hardly consistent with these values. If you can't play within the rules, why would anyone trust you to make the world a better place? Think about the intention of academic policies around plagiarism, cheating, and dishonesty, then consider the benefits of adhering to them.

BENEFITS OF ACADEMIC HONESTY:

- Reflects positive level of integrity; harmony between values and action
- Inspires the pleasure of earning your grades and having them reflective of your effort
- Honors the academic integrity of your college
- Allows you to feel good about yourself
- Reinforces the self-image of high personal character standards
- Shows self-discipline and self-control
- Honors other community members

Take a moment to honor yourself and college career by completing the following statement reflective of your values and commitment to academic integrity.

ACADEMIC INTEGRITY PLEDGE

I promise to never cheat throughout my college career. I make this pledge because I care about my education, character and being a valued member of this community. I will not disgrace my family, those who care about me, trust me and know me. I am better than cheating, lying, faking it or misrepresenting my work. I also pledge... _____

_____
_____
_____
_____
_____
_____
_____

Respectively submitted on _____

by _____

The excuse, "But, I didn't know that was cheating…" will never cross your lips, if you learn the following definitions:

plagiarism (noun): the practice of taking someone else's work or ideas and passing them off as one's own

cheat (verb): act dishonestly or unfairly in order to gain an advantage, especially on an exam

fabricate (verb): invent or concoct (something), typically with deceitful intent; as in making up research

The same technology that helps students plagiarize helps professors catch them with software designed to analyze writing and find words that match associated papers and research already completed. Penalties for academic dishonesty range from a zero on an exam to expulsion from the college or university. Is it worth cutting corners to lower your content of character?

DON'T TAKE SHORTCUTS.

The internet has opened up a whole new world of temptation. It's easy to "borrow" or buy a term paper and thereby use someone else's writing and research. Does that make you a college student or a thief? Even if you don't get caught, you're robbing yourself of the opportunity to learn how to do research, prioritize content, and learn subject matter you might come to love. You will also never learn the skills of writing, efficiency, organization of thoughts, outlining, and putting complex information into understandable content. Shortcuts catch up with you. Be more self-reliant by anticipating the amount of preparation required to write papers, do projects and class assignments. Work backwards from the deadline. If you don't know how to calculate this on your own, talk to your professors at the start of each semester. Be a real college student.

There's no substitute for preparation. It's hard to be prepared for all of your course work. Rudy Giuliani, former mayor of NYC and author of *Leadership*, says in order to be successful "prepare relentlessly." Substitute the temptation (or need) to cheat with effective time management, planning and organizational skills. When your work piles up, you feel overloaded or are afraid you will fail, it's easy to understand how even the most honest of students consider "borrowing" work to prevent the worst from happening. Don't act on it. Instead, take control of your destiny through better preparation.

THINKING PAD

Question to Ask: What are the benefits of doing my own work?

_____
_____
_____
_____
_____
_____
_____
_____
_____
_____
_____

AVOID BLAMING YOUR PROFESSORS.

Hopefully, these scenarios are exceptions: You don't respect your professor, he or she doesn't speak English well, and you essentially hate the way he or she teaches the course. Maybe, you find yourself with a professor who assigns the same work every year, or gives the same exams. Even though these are all tempting reasons to do less than your best, or take a few shortcuts, they are not "good enough" reasons. They are excuses. For instance, if you are shopping for clothes and the salesperson is inattentive, does this give you the right to walk out of the store with items you didn't pay for? No.

Part of growing up is realizing you can't blame anyone but yourself when *you* choose to cheat. Work with (not against) your professors. If you can't understand them, spend more (not less) time with them during their office hours so you learn through personal conversation how to better interpret their speech patterns, dialect and linguistic preferences. If you can't get excited about going to class, sit in the front row. Do what *you* need to do to better engage yourself.

LOOK FOR THE RATIONALE BEHIND ASSIGNMENTS AND REQUIRED COURSES.

"I never wanted to take this stupid writing course anyway… what a waste of time." When you hear these words coming out of your mouth, stop and ask, "What value does this course have in making me a well-rounded and contributing member of society?" Your upperclassmen friends will begrudgingly admit these same general education classes (or core requirements) taught them important lessons, helped them perform better in their majors, or influenced them to completely switch majors. Not seeing the worth of an assignment or entire course doesn't justify bending the rules or finding ways to "beat the system." Your behavior is your behavior, regardless of whether you like the subject matter or believe the class is not relevant to your major.

In other words, look beyond today. By the time you graduate from college, what you thought was a "colossal waste of time" might just come in handy!

PUT GRADES IN PERSPECTIVE.

What's the significance of an academic grade? Essentially, college grades (usually on a 1.0 to 4.0 scale) represent an assessment of the quality of your class work; the level at which you completed course objectives. If you take someone else's work, your grade is a reflection of *their* qualities not your qualities. Acting like you've achieved something you didn't is not responsible. Instead, it reflects immaturity and unethical behavior. In addition, future employers or graduate schools, expect your GPA to reflect your academic achievement and aptitude in comparison to other students. Let them know the real you. Your act of deception contradicts the building of your character. A grade is a grade, but your character will always remain.

Step away from a potential poor grade, and consider the worst thing that can happen as a result of doing your own work and taking the consequences. Then, think of the best consequences.

THINKING PAD

Question to Ask: What have I tried to get out of that ended up adding value to my life?

_____

_____

_____

_____

_____

_____

_____

_____

_____

_____

Question to Ask: What activity or assignment do I have now that I dislike, but will most likely teach me something?

_____

_____

_____

_____

_____

_____

_____

_____

_____

_____

Chapter 19

NOW FACTOR THIRTEEN

CHARACTER ALWAYS COUNTS

"Tell the truth, all of the time. It's the best long term approach, always."

Dr. Dennis R. Black, Vice President for Student Affairs
University at Buffalo, New York

Remember wherever you go, there you are.

Harry Potter had his invisible cloak and some college students have their baseball caps which they wear to class believing, "If I can't see the professor, she can't see me." Unlike Harry, you can be seen. In fact, wherever you go, there you are!

What is it you want others to see when they look at you, or think about you when you are not there? Being someone of character involves becoming someone who possesses the following traits.

Good Character Traits:

- Desire to be a contributing member of society
- Interest in the welfare of others
- Intellectual curiosity
- Willingness to change
- Acceptance and welcoming of constructive feedback
- Honesty
- Predictability (or consistency) of behaviors
- Strong work ethic
- Sense of right and work
- Spirit of inquiry
- Compassion for others
- Concern for the advancement of all mankind
- Civil skills of communication
- Treating others with respect

Peers, professors and potential friends, will know you by your actions – not your words. All day, every day, and for the rest of your life, what you do will speak louder than what you say. Spend time thinking (and writing) about how you want to be seen by others. Who do you want to see when you look in the mirror?

THINKING PAD

Question to ask: What do I want others to see when they see me?

_____

_____

_____

_____

_____

_____

_____

_____

APOLOGIZE WHEN YOU ARE WRONG.

Saying "I'm sorry" will always open more doors than saying, "I'm right." At the end of the day, what will be more important to you; growing in a particular relationship or potentially closing the door on it? Those who insist on being "right" all the time are wrong most of the time. As an emerging adult and human being, you are expected to make mistakes. When you do, apologize. Learn to admit you messed up and then move on.

Sometimes, when you do apologize to someone, it's not enough for them. Despite your sincere attempt to make things better, the damage has been done, they need more time, or they simply don't have the capacity to forgive you. In these situations, you can keep trying, be patient or "let it go." When you choose the last option, it may mean the relationship is also over. That's not always a bad thing. Be willing to "let it go."

It is possible, however, what you did, didn't do, said, or failed to say, hurt someone deeper than you think, or reeked more havoc than you realize. In these situations, you should consider "letting go" of your self-righteousness, lack of compassion, self-centeredness, self-pride or arrogance. One of the greatest difficulties in apologizing is often realizing just how wrong *you* might have been. The act of apologizing is not only for someone else's sake, but for your own.

WAYS TO SAY "I'M SORRY":

- Say "I'm sorry."
- Send a card with a hand written apology. Never apologize via email (that's cold.)
- Set up a coffee date and admit your mistake in person.
- Make a phone call that begins, "I am an idiot..." followed by your apology.
- Do a random act of kindness to someone you've hurt.
- Ease someone's burden by offering a sincere compliment after you apologize.
- Remember everyone has their own "story" and life isn't always fair.
- Change your behaviors. They will notice.
- Make something right that you wronged even if it cost you something to do so.

ATTEND LEADERSHIP DEVELOPMENT OPPORTUNITIES.

Time and time again you will overhear aspiring, competent and high achieving college students invite other students (maybe you) to accompany them to one of the numerous leadership conferences offered on campus or training programs open to all students. Unfortunately, you will also overhear the invitee's response, "Why would I want to do that?" Listen to your own sound judgment telling you to attend!

By taking advantage of the many leadership training and personal development programs on your campus, you will receive (free of charge) what corporations spend millions of dollars to provide for their employees. You don't need to be in a student organization or have a position of leadership to attend either. You can just show up! To find out what training opportunities have been scheduled on your campus, visit your student activities office, center for student involvement, or community outreach office, check into your online course catalogue or search the college website.

The kinds of opportunities available will vary. There are the formal courses, sometimes called First Year Experience courses, Introduction to Leadership Theory, or Leadership 101 which offer academic credit. There are also leadership series, workshops hosted in your residence hall, and online programs offered through your college's website. By taking advantage of such opportunities, you become exposed to various definitions of leadership, get the chance to do self-assessments, meet like-minded peers and pick up new skills. Instead of having to figure out how to become a more competent individual all on your own, leadership training shortens the learning curve! Which of the following skill sets would come in handy?

LEADERSHIP DEVELOPMENT FACILITATES...

- Having a conversation
- Dealing with difficult people
- Organization and energy management
- Working effectively in groups
- Building healthy relationships
- Staying well and fit
- Growing in faith
- Managing stress
- Finding the motivation from within
- Helping others

- Building personal self-esteem
- Communicating to be understood
- Learning how to be assertive
- Motivating others
- Knowing your strengths and weaknesses

TREAT OTHERS WITH RESPECT.

To *have* a good friend, you need to *be* a good friend. This theory holds true for many qualities, including respect. When you feel worthy of being respected, you will respect others. Until that time arrives, practice respecting others.

Given the deluge of "reality TV" it's hard to define "respect." You can watch hours of people demeaning other people, cutting each other off during mid-sentence and screaming to make a point. Some call this "entertainment." In actuality, you are witnessing a complete disregard for basic human rights. One of which is the right to be treated with respect.

Is respect earned? Yes. Should it be offered whether it is earned or not? Yes. When you show respect to someone, you are making a statement about your positive character. Specifically, you are giving people the benefit of the doubt, demonstrating through your actions and words that you are considerate, and putting other's needs ahead of your own. It often takes more time and care to be respectful than it does to make your world revolve solely around you.

What does respect look like? If you were to break down all the behaviors around respect, you would notice not only a long list, rather a diversity of behaviors. *Respect* is not that complicated, it's the act of showing consideration of others. When you believe you are worthy of consideration (also characterized by high self-esteem) you will know how to respect yourself, and others.

ASSIGNMENT: **RESPECT**

Directions: You have an opportunity to grade yourself on the following list of respect indicators. Use a 4.0 scale (1.0 = "D" and 4.0 = "A") and grade yourself on each item. Add up all of your scores and divide by 20. Did you pass?

_____ Acknowledging those you meet with a "hello"

_____ Never raising your voice to someone unless it's a safety issue

_____ Sending someone a thank you card if they do something nice for you

_____ Returning phone calls within 24 hours

_____ Arriving on time to appointments

_____ Showing up if you say you will show up

_____ Honoring your commitments

_____ Adhering to established laws and policies

_____ Not interrupting someone while they are speaking

_____ Waiting to eat until everyone else is served

_____ Demonstrating proper dinner etiquette

_____ Being a team player

_____ Listening to other's advice (doesn't mean you have to take it...)

_____ Saying "thank you" when someone spends their energy to make you happy

_____ Offering to help

_____ Being honest and telling the truth

_____ Cleaning up after yourself so others don't have to

_____ Not being disruptive in quiet areas

_____ Allowing others to accomplish their goals

_____ Not using profanity or offensive language

ASK YOURSELF THE TOUGH QUESTIONS.

Becoming a decent human being is work. There will be moments at the "mountain top" and times when you wallow in the "valley of despair" (to quote Dr. Martin Luther King, Jr.) – and, there will be questioning moments. Which words below represent the goal of higher education?

Inquiry
Curiosity
Intrigue
Mystery
Challenge
Questions
Exploration

That's right! All of the above! These notions will build your character by forcing you to self-examine and self-inspect. You don't need to have the answers. It's the practice of *asking* the questions that will help you through the tough times, identify your mistakes and achievements, recognize the results of your choices, and help you to grow up, become smarter and build your content of character.

The next time you find yourself staring off into space, pick up a writing implement and try to answer some of the following questions:

When am I at my best?
What decision(s) have I made in my life I most regret?
When did I realize there were people in this world who have so much less than I do?
What was the deciding factor in my decision to go to college?
Who have I harmed the most in my life?

Where would I travel if I could go anywhere in the world?
What's the most "transparent" part of my personality?
How do I pick my friends?
What qualities do I value in others?
When do I not tell the truth the most?
When I was five years old, what did I want to become?
Who has had the greatest positive influence in my life?
What are the five things I should be proud of?

STAND UP FOR WHAT IS RIGHT.

In the game of Simon Says, the only one left standing is Simon. That's how the game is played. Despite Simon's ability to trick you, wear you down and distract you from oppressive self-serving motives, you enjoyed playing the game as a child because it was fun.

The real life version of Simon Says will speak directly to you. Listen carefully. Simon will be disguised as well-intentioned do-gooders, corporate leaders, intellectuals, and politicians. Simon will also appear to you in the form of "beer, peer and fear pressure." Don't be fooled.

When you become more knowing and develop sound reasoning skills, the only thing stopping you from doing the right thing is courage. College is a laboratory of learning. Practice the art of protecting other's basic human rights, advocate for those without a voice, confront someone who is engaging in harmful behaviors, and tell Simon to sit down. If not now, when?

"In Germany, they first came for the Communists and I didn't speak up because I wasn't a Communist. Then they came for the Jews and I didn't speak up because I wasn't a Jew. Then they came for the trade unionists and I didn't speak up because I wasn't a trade unionist. Then they came for the Catholics and I didn't speak up because I was a Protestant. Then they came for me – and by that time no one was left to speak up."

- Pastor Martin Niemoller

Chapter 20

NOW FACTOR FOURTEEN

YOU CAN BE SMART AND STUPID AT THE SAME TIME

"Date people smarter than you. It will improve your GPA."

Jake Denney, student
Tufts University, Medford, Massachusetts

IDENTIFY YOUR CORE VALUES AND MORALS.

Remember when your parent or guardian told you what was right or wrong? They most likely still do! But through learning what was right or wrong, you began to define your own values and morals.

Have you ever taken a moment to write down what it is you believe in? And what you value? You may know exactly how to respond to those questions, or you may need some time to think them through. *Values* and *morals* represent your internal belief system and ultimately define you. They make up the foundation from which you make decisions and live your life.

An easy way to determine your morals and values is by finishing the statement, "I live my life by..." followed by the traits and teachings that guide you. Use the blanks below to explore what composes your very being.

THINKING PAD

Question to Ask: What do I value?

_____

_____

_____

_____

Question to Ask: What do I consider to be in my moral toolbox?

_____

_____

_____

_____

Question to Ask: How do I know that these are my values and morals?

_____

_____

_____

_____

SAY "NO!" TO PEER PRESSURE.

Do you remember when your friend dared you to do something and you knew deep down it would be something that would get you in trouble? Because you didn't know how to voice your opposition, you heard the word, "Yes!" come out of your mouth? Ever literally close your eyes with the prayer, "If I can't see myself doing this, I must not be doing it!?!" You were grounded.

Being in college will expose you to new people and new situations causing you to make decisions instantly. Situations from your youth will immediately pop into your head, sending conflicting messages. Not everything you will be asked to do by your "friends" will be the right thing to do. Practicing how to say, "No!" is a challenge, but one you can master!

College is an environment where you will have to make smart decisions which may upset your friends. Avoid upsetting yourself or letting yourself down by going along with something you don't want to do. Activities around alcohol and drugs are good examples of peer pressure situations requiring you to stop and reflect on your morals and values. If a particular activity, or potential outcome, isn't on your list of things to do, it's OK to walk away or answer in the negative. Remember, your reputation will arrive before you do!

KNOW YOUR LIMITS.

How do you know when you've gone too far? When is "enough" actually more than enough? With all the freedom and independence accompanying this time of life, comes the potential for exercising poor judgment. You are now being expected to behave and think at a higher level of maturity, and maintain your membership in a community committed to high standards of personal conduct, civility and intellectual growth. When do you know what isn't acceptable?

A good barometer for determining whether or not you should proceed down a certain path or need a "reality check" is to have an internal dialogue *before* you act. When you have to ask, "What was I thinking?" it's too late. If you find yourself calling a coach for bail money, you've probably taken it too far. Being removed from your residence hall pretty much puts the exclamation point on your lack of judgment.

There are a variety of consequences for *not* knowing your limits, ranging from serious physical harm to yourself or others, to literally being kicked out of school. Taking the time to explore the following questions *before* you act is a wise move.

THE IMPORTANT QUESTIONS:

Is this illegal?
Will I potentially wreck my reputation or help it?
What will my friends think differently of me after this?
How does this reflect upon my leadership?
Is this dangerous?
Can I harm someone else?
Could this kill me?
Do I know of others who have been hurt doing this?

Why do I feel uncomfortable or is this the right thing to do?
Is my self-respect being challenged or upheld?
Who would be disappointed or pleased by this action?
Am I respecting or disrespecting someone?
Do the benefits outweigh the cost?

Knowing your limits involves saying, "Yes" and "No." When you have studying to do, you need to say, "No" to going to the movies. When you are struggling with an assignment, you need to say, "Yes" to your professor when she asks you to stop by during office hours. Getting in touch with your strengths and weaknesses is part of college. In the meantime, stay within the margins of safety, legal activity and wisdom.

DRINK IN MODERATION OR NOT AT ALL.

You might find it hard to believe more students on a college campus don't drink than do drink! If you are not comfortable consuming alcohol, you are not alone. Number one, it is against the law if you are under 21. Number two, an increasing number of young adults going into college choose not to drink, or drink in moderation. They prefer the "substance-free" life-style.

With the consumption of alcohol comes a variety of physical responses. Some of these responses are rather humorous, and when taken too far, are dangerous and life threatening. Drinking socially (one beer per hour or less) in the company of friends is a mature way of having a good time without taking it too far. When you begin to feel out of control, it's time to put down the beverage and switch to water.

Many students show up to social events with their own "beverage of choice." Usually this is a water bottle or soda. What's going to be your choice?

There are policies on every campus about underage drinking. Let's be real — it still happens. You get to decide, however, how *you* want to socialize. Choosing not to drink is totally acceptable.

Caution! Binge drinking is dangerous. When you've had a really rough day, failed an exam or received bad news from home, going out to drink is usually not a smart move. *Binge drinking* is a rapid over consumption of alcohol that begins with the intent of "getting wasted." Students learn quickly after a night of their face in a toilet (sounds disgusting, doesn't it?) that binge drinking can produce unpleasant physical reactions.

SIGNS IT'S TIME TO SWITCH TO WATER:

- When the room starts to sway
- When your stomach begins to do cartwheels
- When you begin to say things you can't take back
- When clothes start coming off
- When you no longer can protect your reputation
- When your judgment is impaired
- When you start to engage in illegal activity
- When you begin to lose control
- When you've already consumed more than a reasonable amount of alcohol

RESPECT YOUR RIGHT (OR THEIR RIGHT) TO NOT HAVE SEX.

It's your body to keep. If you don't want to engage in risky behaviors — that's your right! Taking care of your body is now your job and responsibility, as if you didn't have enough to do! But, as a college student it's important to realize you aren't a cat with nine lives. There are serious consequences to living dangerously, including potential damage to your reputation. That's why now is the time to pay attention to your mind, body and spirit. How are you treating them?

Whether or not to engage in sexual relations is a personal choice and it's *your* choice. This decision should never be made "in the moment." Considerable advance thought is necessary to avoid life-altering consequences.

QUESTIONS TO CONTEMPLATE BEFORE HAVING SEX:

- What do my religious beliefs tell me about having sex?
- How does having a sexual relationship fit my moral beliefs?
- Do I want to save myself for marriage?
- Is this relationship a committed relationship?
- How do I know I'm not the "only one?"
- When he or she says "they've got protection," how can I be sure?
- Would he or she lie about their previous sexual encounters?
- What would I do if she got pregnant?
- How is my reputation going to be affected?
- How well do I really know this person?
- Am I getting in over my head – can I handle the emotional stress?
- If I think he or she will leave if I don't have sex, is this the right relationship to begin with?
- What if he or she has a sexually transmitted disease?
- How much do I really know about what I'm doing?
- How will I feel if this is the first and last time with this person?
- Is there anything wrong with waiting until the relationship is stronger or just saying, "No?"

DON'T WALK AROUND AT NIGHT ALONE.

Be safe. Overall, college and university campuses are safe places and have more than adequate security and police coverage. But, they are still accessible to individuals with less than good intentions. Unfortunately, as we've seen in recent history, some of these dangerous people are classmates. You always want to be on your guard and be smart.

Read everything about safety, security and emergency response policies provided by your university and college. Know evacuation routes, fire and emergency numbers, and what to do when alarms go off. This information is available on your college's website. You also want to do smart things on a regular basis to keep you safe.

SMART SAFETY MOVES:

- Never walk out to your car alone.
- Park your car under well lit areas.
- Walk along designated pathways.
- Be aware of where "call boxes" or "blue lights" are located.
- Carry your cell phone when jogging off campus.
- Never jog down wooded paths and parks alone.
- Lock your car as soon as you get in it.
- Leave your residence hall room locked at night.
- Don't prop doors open that have automatic locks – that's for a reason.
- Never drink and drive – call someone.
- Don't walk home alone after drinking.
- Let someone know where you are going.
- Leave your roommate a note if you are going out late.
- Stay away from drunk or impaired people you don't know.
- Never leave a drink unattended.
- When in doubt – trust your gut. Be smart.

SEEK COMPATIBLE AND SUPPORTIVE RELATIONSHIPS.

College seems like a good time to meet people, even that "special someone." However, anyone you meet needs to understand that you (and maybe them, too) are in college to get an education, which should be your *top* priority. If you are just going to college to meet someone, perhaps you shouldn't be in college at all. This isn't to say casual dating, hanging out with friends, and socializing aren't important parts of your college experience; these are things that need to be kept in the proper perspective.

It may sound silly, but the people you might date are like elevators: they either take you up or down. Some will demand all of your time, others will understand your need to do homework, study for exams, and invest in your college success. It's important to be compatible with your friends and significant others, so these relationships don't come at the expense of your work and school goals. Be sure the people in your life understand your purpose, vision and goals!

When getting to know someone, share your goals with them so you can determine whether this is a person who is counterproductive to your college experience or someone who will encourage and support your involvements and priorities. You'll need to communicate your needs (must haves) and your wants (things you like but you're flexible on these.) You'll also want to share your expectations (what you are looking for in a partner and friend) as you get to know others. It's often difficult to build relationships when your mind should be on college. Be sure to ride the elevator up!

"Advice is seldom welcome,
and those who need it most
like it least."

- Samuel Johnson

Random Thoughts...

Chapter 21

NOW FACTOR FIFTEEN

LOVE MAKES THE WORLD GO ROUND

"A nation, as a society, forms a moral person, and every member of it is personally responsible for his society."

Thomas Jefferson

Love yourself first.

When you look in the mirror, do you like who looks back? There will be days as a college student you won't even recognize the reflection. What you will see is a work in progress. That's a good thing. There will also be days when you look in the mirror and see nothing but greatness! In fact, the reflection might utter, "Looking good, my friend, looking good!"

You don't have to always *like* yourself, but try to always *love* yourself. When you become frustrated, or do something you wish you hadn't, love yourself enough to work through it and move on. At any given moment you can change a behavior or an attitude. Love yourself enough to try. Don't become defensive or have a pity party where you are the only invited guest! Don't play the blame game or act like Teflon where nothing ever "sticks" on you. Love yourself enough to know the difference between a behavior (which is changeable) and your content of character.

Ways to Remember How to Love Yourself:

- Treat yourself to a study break.
- Contact a special friend.
- Admit your mistakes, apologize and move on.
- Pick yourself some flowers.
- Sit in the sun, feel the warmth on your face, and smile.
- Count your blessings in the shower every morning.
- Keep a list of everything you like about yourself.
- Take the right kind of risks to expand your talents.
- Share your talents with those less fortunate.
- Work out on a daily basis.
- Send yourself a card.
- Ask for what you need.
- Compliment yourself in the mirror every day.
- Only hang out with quality friends.

SEEK ROMANTIC RELATIONSHIPS BASED UPON MUTUAL RESPECT.

Dating in college is considerably different than high school. The most obvious difference is the absence of an authority figure (i.e. parent or guardian) looking over your shoulder. What you want from your dating relationships and how you conduct yourself is entirely up to you now.

The social scene on campus, involvement in student organizations, attending class, or going to study in the library, all offer opportunities to meet new people, including someone you'd be interested in dating. The dilemma for today's college student, however, is how to define "dating."

Dating is not "hooking up." *Dating* suggests a tad more advance thought on your part and the desire to spend time with someone who makes you a better person. Stay away from needy possessive jealous partners who are all consuming and aren't secure in who they are so they need you to make them "whole." Yucko. Enjoy this time in your life by enjoying relationships based on positive mutual regard, effective communication and fun.

THE LOOK OF HEALTHY RELATIONSHIPS:

- Respect for the other's commitments
- Not setting unrealistic "rules" or expectations
- Being able to communicate without fear of judgment
- Spending time together in groups of friends
- Attending events together
- Speaking only positively of others to your friends
- Never raising your voice during disagreements
- Giving each other the space to be a student or work
- Not calling each other names or swearing at each other

- Laughing together
- Feeling appreciated and valued
- Thinking of each other when you're not together
- Supporting each other's dreams and goals
- Not crossing the lines of intimacy if it's not mutual
- Enjoying being together because it's easy

Dating takes time. Do you have it? You will have many things competing for your time, and often romantic relationships take more time than you can afford. They can also take more emotional energy, commitment and money than you can afford as a college student! That's why many college students don't date, but prefer to establish meaningful friendships where there is less stress and pressure. Not to forget, the love between friends usually lasts longer!

BE THERE FOR OTHERS.

Showing those around you the capacity for understanding, compassion and empathy is a sign of enhanced growth and maturity. It's what college students do very well. The freedom to become a better you comes with better vision; what you used to *not* notice in others becomes recognizable as pain, loneliness, discomfort, and hurt.

Everyone has a story. You have a story. The stress and business of college life sometimes makes it hard to stop long enough and act on what you can now see – peers who need your friendship, kindness and attention. If you have ever been made to feel "invisible," as if someone can see right through you, it's not hard to grasp the value in being there for your classmates, teammates, fellow new students and the strangers who are making up your college community.

You are connected to those around you with many of the same

feelings, realities and aspirations. You all want essentially the same things. You also have many of the same stressors and pressures causing you (and your classmates) to occasionally freak out, lash out, retreat, call home or act like you are six years old! *Empathy* is the ability to walk in someone else's shoes. You can do that! You are doing that! Before you speak negatively of someone ask yourself, "Why might they be feeling this way and have I been there, too?"

Being a person of compassion is a good thing. It makes you likeable, approachable and a contributor to your college community. Compassion comes from love for others. There are many ways to show compassion in college. See if any of the ideas below fit your personality. Practice will make perfect!

THE LOOK OF COMPASSION:

- Asking how someone is and waiting around for the answer
- Spending extra time with someone who needs a friend
- Following up with someone you know has had a bad day
- Offering up a warm hug
- Admitting that "life can be hard" instead of saying "it will all work out"
- Bringing someone a candy bar or treat to cheer them up and let them know you know
- Saying "I'm here"
- Showing up without being asked

QUIT FRIENDSHIPS THAT AREN'T SERVING YOU WELL.

"I quit you," are tough words, but sometimes necessary to say in order to keep your circle of support and inspiration reflective of who you want to be and your needs. You will be known by your associations and greatly influenced by your interactions with them. Care about who you spend your time with. Which friendships, teammates, and study partners bring you the most joy? As an adult, it's up to you to take inventory of the people around you and their potential impact on your happiness, growth and future.

Proximity. Unfortunately, that's often the criteria for the making of many a college friendship and relationship. Your initial social circles will often be formed based upon the "convenience of contact." When students live next door to each other or play on the same team, the frequency of contact is greater which often leads to more conversation, the making of plans and hanging out. If you have to walk all the way down the hall to meet someone, or schedule a get together, more effort is required! Because it can often take weeks and months to be comfortable with someone, you have to assume it's worth the cost and time. It often is!

Try not to take the easy way out! Expend some energy to get to know people who bring you up, appear interesting, and have high standards and similar values. Choose them over the more convenient next door neighbor who zaps all of your energy or has opposing values. Go for *quality* of friendships over *quantity*.

Once you get to know someone, you might discover you really don't care for them or your relationship. Said another way, you would prefer to spend your time differently. This is a sign of maturity and shows you can be kind to others without having to be around people just for the sake of being around people.

There are many reasons for "quitting friendships." You don't have to be someone's "emotional punching bag;" where they take their frustrations out on you because they know you will keep coming back for more. You don't have to be someone's "convenient friend" either; where they seek you out when no one else is available. You don't have to be taken advantage of, talked about behind your back or made to feel like someone's "personal counselor;" where it's always about their "issues" and never about enjoying your company.

From the inside out, you will know when it's time to say to another person, "You know, I am not feeling valued in our friendship and think I need to spend time pursuing other things." You can also say this with your actions by not being available as often, or inviting someone you want to get to know better to do something with you. Asking a group if you can join them the next time they go out, or finding other ways to spend your time like going to a sporting event, taking yourself to a movie, and seeking a good bookstore, are all ways to expand your social circle. Enjoy finding *quality* friends over *quantity*!

Did You Know?

Sheryl Crow, the musician and activist, was a resident assistant at the University of Missouri at Columbia.

"In a time of social
fragmentation, vulgarity
becomes a way of life.
To be shocking becomes
important – and often more
profitable – than to be civil or
creative or truly original."

- Al Gore

Random Thoughts...

Chapter 22

NOW FACTOR SIXTEEN

WHEN YOUR TANK IS EMPTY YOU CAN'T DRIVE FAR

"Use your college experiences to develop a niche – something you're good at that you can evidence to others."

Dr. Kevin P. Simpson, Professor of Medicine
Loyola University of Chicago, Illinois

Recalculate your need to consume food.

Accompanying the reality you are about to run out of gas are feelings of nervousness, sweat on your brow, and anxiousness in the pit of your stomach. Every bump in the road and rattling noise underscores the "E" on your dashboard. You are very aware of the possibility of getting in trouble.

Your stomach is like a fuel tank. It is designed to run off of a certain amount of calories a day, prefers premium fuel to low leaded options, and if you overfill it at the pump, it still only holds comfortably what it holds; the rest ends up on the pavement! When you forget to add fuel during the day, your body responds with a headache, growling stomach, irritability and awareness you *may* get stuck.

You will start to experience an adjustment period in your eating habits the minute you walk on campus. Instead of having your meals at a regular time and place, your schedule will be filled with the unexpected and there will be much greater demands on your time. The amount and variety of food available to you will most likely increase tremendously with "all you can eat" options everywhere. Before you know it, your clothes begin to feel tight and you've put on the infamous "freshmen fifteen!" You begin to wonder if anything will ever fit again.

The balancing act between going to class, studying, working, and involvement in campus organizations, for instance, also makes it more difficult to prioritize healthy eating behaviors. Without realizing it, your tank hits "E" at critical points in your day! Now you *are* stuck.

To avoid relying on fumes for energy, or putting on (or dropping) too much weight, eat enough to make you feel content and not stuffed. The "all you can eat" buffet is always going to be there. Give thought to what you feel like eating and pick one meal not four. Just because you can eat a cheeseburger, bowl of spaghetti, order of French fries, cereal, loaf of bread, and sundae in one sitting doesn't make it a good idea!

Skipping meals isn't the best response to your new life style, either. Smaller portions of vegetables, carbs, fruit and proteins, eaten at least three times a day, will keep your energy levels up. When you skip breakfast, you literally are starting your day on empty! How far do you expect to get?

Stay SHARP.

Staying healthy in college means staying "SHARP," so you have the energy to participate in all of the opportunities you desire. You should want to feel and look your best, which isn't as hard as you think with the following strategy:

Sharp Strategy

Small Meals Often: To stay fueled and have the energy you need to get through the day, eat a number of small meals or snacks all day long versus one big meal late at night. Try to incorporate a mixture of carbohydrates (like bread, fruits and vegetables) and proteins (like meats and legumes.) As a guide, if you get really hungry, you've waited too long between eating. Plan each day with a good number of "mini-meals" in mind. Don't forget to drink at least 6 to 8 glasses (8 ounces) of water a day!

Highly Nutritious: A candy bar, bag of popcorn or box of Altoids, do not qualify as "nutritious" snacks. Make your small meals count for something. Choose lean meats like turkey, chicken or fish. Select fresh fruits and salads with low calorie and low fat dressing. Vary your choices by changing up the color of your food selections! You might also consider taking a daily multi-vitamin.

(By the way… alcohol counts as "empty calories," not as your daily carbohydrate requirement!) To stay fueled (and maintain a healthy weight) your goal is to get the most nutrition from every calorie consumed, therefore, limit junk food and your alcohol consumption. Start paying attention to how you fuel your energy.

Active Movement: Don't you find it ironic how the expenditure of energy through exercise actually gives you energy? Students who have a daily exercise routine consistently report greater energy levels, enhanced memory recall, and more studying efficiency. There's no replacement for a daily movement routine that gives you enjoyment. You don't have to lift weights or be strapped to a treadmill. Go for a walk, dance to your favorite music, do aerobics, or sign up for a PE class. To maximize the benefits of a daily fitness routine, your goal is no less than thirty minutes of active movement which raises your heart beat, stretches your muscles and improves your breathing.

Regular Sleep: What does getting enough sleep have to do with keeping fuel in your tank? When you don't get enough sleep, you are more likely to either eat too much or eat the wrong food. You will find yourself irritable, more easily stressed and prone to illness (due to a lowered immune system). Although you don't want to hear what comes next, take note: Research consistently notes college-aged students require 6 to 8 hours of sleep per night (not per week) to maintain intellectual acuity, manage stress and stay healthy! That may seem unrealistic, but it doesn't change the need your body has for sleep!

Plan for Indulgences: Pizza! Ice cream! All you can eat BBQ wings! Vending machine raids at 2 a.m.! You can still stay "SHARP" by partaking in the occasional splurge, especially if you "calculate" them into your week ahead of time. Try to limit yourself to one or two "indulgences" per week. When will you be up late studying? Are you going out over the weekend? Is someone having a party?

You might have to pass on the early week candy bar, go with more salads, work out faithfully and be prepared to demonstrate some self-discipline. It's your body!

It's time for a personal dialogue. How would you answer the following questions?

How do I feel about eating smaller portions more often?
What nutritious foods do I find delicious?
What foods should I eat more of to stay fit?
What exercises or energy exertion do I most enjoy?
How many hours of sleep do I require to be well rested?
What are the things that stop me from getting enough sleep?
How can I get enough sleep?
What food items do I consume out of proper portion?

Benefits of staying SHARP!:

- Staying power and energized
- Healthy outlook on life and enhanced appearance
- Accountability and sense of control
- Real practice in developing lifelong habits of wellness
- Permission to have some fun and "cut loose" once in awhile

FOCUS ON THE POSITIVE OUTCOMES OF TAKING PROPER CARE OF YOURSELF.

You will get smarter in college – at least that's the theory. One significant sign of your enhanced intelligence will be the priority you place on taking care of *all* aspects of your continued development, not just one. If you were to "grade" how well you've done so far, would you pass with flying colors? Do you only think about thinking, or are you in charge of your *whole being*?

COMPONENTS OF CARE:

- Spiritual development
- Physical conditioning
- Emotional stability
- Psychological health
- Recreational endeavors
- Functional social relationships (support systems)
- Overall physical fitness
- Intellectual stimulation
- Prevention of illness
- Management of stress

One of the greatest gifts a college education will give you is the opportunity to get what you want out of life and create your future. Your body is going to go where you go. You do get to control whether it works with you or against you! Consider the perks of having the fuel you need when you need it!

THE PERKS OF A FULL TANK:

- You'll be more fun to be around.
- You'll be able to persevere through the difficult times.
- You'll be less likely to fall asleep during class.
- You'll go to class.
- You'll appear more positive to those around you.
- You'll have people around you.
- You'll have healthy hair and skin.
- You'll look good and feel more attractive.
- You'll exhibit more self-confidence.
- You'll be more willing to ask someone out.
- You'll be better equipped to deal.
- You'll live better and longer.

- You'll get sick less often.
- You'll be sharper and remember more.
- You'll have the time to be spontaneous.
- You'll get through late night study sessions.
- You'll manage a healthy weight.
- You'll demonstrate your ability to take care of yourself – all of you!

AVOID ALL-NIGHTERS.

What happens when you have too much to do and run out of time… all-nighters! At first, the concept makes sense; you need to finish a project, type a term paper or study for finals. Because you didn't plan in advance, the deadline has approached and you're not as prepared as you should be. You begin to keep putting off what you know is quickly approaching, and talk yourself into the myth, "I'll stay up all night if I have to get it done!" Bad plan.

Pulling an "all-nighter" is actually a plan to *not* plan. It is the outcome of poor organization and inadequate time management. Nothing you are assigned should come as a surprise because your course syllabus has given you "advance notice." That's why counting backwards from deadlines, exams and project presentations, allows you adequate preparation time. Not only will the quality of your work be significantly better, but your mental functioning won't be compromised. What good is it to study throughout the night for your final, only to mess with the chemicals in your brain (via sleep deprivation) to the point you aren't able to recall any information by the time you sit for the exam?

ASK FOR HELP WHEN YOU NEED IT.

There are professionals on every university and college campus whose sole job is to make sure you are OK. When you feel alone, down, confused or desperate, you need to ask someone for help who is trained to get you the proper resources, listen in confidence and provide guidance or counseling. A good place to start is by talking with your residence director ("RD") if you feel comfortable, or by visiting the counseling center on campus.

Don't be embarrassed or ashamed if you are having trouble navigating new territory or dealing with personal issues. At one point or another, most college students experience situations requiring another set of ears, advice and support. Whether your difficulties stem from situations at home, roommate conflicts, academic pressure or challenges meeting people, take advantage of the professional support system in place. Your tuition dollars have already paid for these services.

If you don't feel like speaking with a professional counselor, you can ask for help from a variety of individuals who will show you unconditional positive regard.

WHERE TO GO FOR HELP:

- Academic advisor
- Professor
- Athletic or club coach
- Student organization advisor
- Counseling center
- Health center
- Resident advisor
- Orientation leader
- Dean of students

Don't wait until minor issues become major ones. Shout loudly! If you need help figuring how to "be a college student" you need help! If you don't know how to study for a particular course, you need help! If you are having problems with your roommate, you need help! Be worthy enough to take care of yourself and get the support you need which often means letting someone know you have questions or are struggling. You are not alone. So, shout loudly… "I need help!"

SAY "NO!" TO BEING HAZED OR HAZING OTHERS.

Did you see Animal House? Much to the dismay of national fraternal organizations, you probably did see the movie. Recognize hazing isn't limited to pledges wanting to join a "frat" house. Hazing is a very real societal problem spanning from high school cheerleading squads to marching bands and from college student organizations to athletic teams.

Although illegal in almost every state, hazing finds its way onto college campuses when individuals falsely believe they have the power, status or authority to subject those without it to do certain things to gain acceptance, membership or status. *Hazing* is a deliberate effort to gain "respect, authority and submissiveness" through humiliating, harassing, threatening, abusive, frightening, life threatening, or absurd tactics. In short, hazing is stupid.

You might have seen or heard of "hazing" in high school. It's wrong wherever it takes place because its very practice is one of "initiation by intimidation." You should never have to "prove" to anyone on a college campus you have what it takes to partici-pate. Your enrollment is enough! All student organizations, clubs, teams and activities are there for you to join – as you are! If you are asked, told or "required" to do any of the following types of activities, you need to say, "No!" and leave immediately.

What seems like a funny "college thing to do" or silly prank, can often turn demeaning, humiliating, and in all too many unfor-tunate cases, deadly. Almost anything can be "hazing" if the ultimate outcome of the activity is unproductive, negative, harmful or intended to superficially earn respect. A list of examples could take pages, so a few are noted below to give you an idea of what *not* to choose to do (and it is a choice) or *not* do to others:

THE LOOK OF HAZING:

- Nudity of any kind
- Mental anguish
- Alcohol or drug consumption
- Skipping academic assignments or class
- Attendance at illegal activities
- Damaging or vandalizing property
- Violating college or university Code of Conduct
- Consuming undesirable food substances
- Taking people against their will
- Breaking the law
- Degrading name calling and language
- Physical demands
- Dangerous activities
- Disruption to sleep patterns

What to do? If you feel uncomfortable about a practice you've heard about (or witnessed) you can act like a grown-up by taking responsibility for your community and not putting yourself in legal or physical risk. Do the right thing. Hazing is illegal. There are penalties for not only those who haze, but for those who *know of it* and don't report it! That's right. If you witness hazing, you are legally required to report it to a university official like your dean of students, or campus police department. Hazing is not a joke and has no place in higher education. You are entitled to a quality education and an equal opportunity to participate in those activities and experiences supported by your tuition dollars and activities fees.

FIND SOURCES OF SPIRITUAL RENEWAL.

What gives you strength from the inside out? Is it your faith? A walk through nature? Time alone in meditation? When you take a few minutes out of your busy schedule to fill up your soul, you will enjoy less stress, more peace and remain in control of your life.

There's no escaping the craziness of being a college student. That's part of the fun! There are new freedoms and new responsibilities. There are new challenges and new ways of creating your future. It's all good, but it's all crazy!

Whether you are a person of faith, or believe in forces greater than you, try not to neglect your internal needs for spiritual renewal. Feed your soul in the years ahead. There are other students with the same needs seeking more formal means of spiritual renewal, like attending a local church or the non-denominational service on campus. You will find numerous student organizations and listings of these types of activities on campus ranging from mediation classes, outing club expeditions, yoga courses, religiously-based choirs, to faith-based organizations or centers.

If you prefer to keep your spiritual journey more private, you can find creative ways to stay spiritually whole, as suggested below.

HOW TO FIND INTERNAL STRENGTH:

- Keep a journal.
- Write a letter to yourself once a week.
- Experiment with writing poetry.
- Attend a worship service.
- Read a book of poetry.
- Listen to songs of nature.

- Talk a long walk in nature (be sure it is a safe area with open spaces).
- Find a space in nature that "speaks to you."
- Pray frequently throughout your day.
- Put on music and dance expressively.
- Go for a long run with a specific destination.
- Say words of affirmation out loud (i.e. "I am loved").
- Listen to soulful music.
- Meditate.

TALK TO YOUR RESIDENT ADVISOR.

Who are these outgoing, upperclassmen who always seem to be busy doing something? The *resident advisor* is your "go-to-person" if you live in a residence hall. They undergo considerable training and extensive selection so they will be there if you need them. Resident advisors (also called "community assistants") are the eyes and ears of your residence hall floor, help report any maintenance or roommate problems, and care about building a sense of community for you to enjoy.

In many cases, the "RA" is a good communicator and listener. When you need to talk with someone your own age, consider a conversation with these dedicated student leaders – you might be pleasantly surprised!

THINKING PAD

Question to Ask: How might I get in touch with my internal spirit and soul? What makes me nervous or excited about focusing on my spiritual development?

_____
_____
_____
_____

_____
_____
_____
_____
_____

Question to Ask: What personal needs might be met by taking
the time to examine what's inside of me and where I can get
internal sources of strength, faith and hope?

_____
_____
_____
_____
_____
_____
_____
_____
_____

"If one is lucky, a solitary fantasy can totally transform one million realities."

- Maya Angelou

Random Thoughts...

Chapter 23

NOW FACTOR SEVENTEEN

LAUGHTER ISN'T ALWAYS THE BEST MEDICINE

"Sleep."

Sharon Broussard, Assistant Director of Student Health
Services
Merrimack College, Massachusetts

KEEP IT ALL IN PERSPECTIVE.

College students get sick. You may wake up one morning feeling miserable, out of it, and just awful. After a trip to the health center or your doctor, you end up with a prescription. When the medicine kicks in, you are back to your healthy self. If you are able to get through college without feeling stress, overwhelmed or sick, you'd not only be considered lucky, but rare! Part of the college experience is learning how to process lots of information and simultaneously manage enormous amounts of work – much of which doesn't fit within the time you've got. Just knowing that feeling overwhelmed is "normal" can provide perspective. But, what can you do to make sure it doesn't ruin your college experience?

You will get through the demands ahead by managing how you spend your time, learning to prioritize, identifying what calms you down, and optimizing healthy ways of reducing stress. Learning to laugh will also serve you well.

Picture this…Your alarm clock doesn't go off, you awake to realize you're late. Rushing out of your room, you reach for your backpack and throw it quickly over your shoulder. The back loop gets caught on your door, opening the zipper and spilling all of your contents on the floor. What is the best response? Laugh, get mad or cry? Laugh.

When you take time to laugh at the silly, crazy, and sometimes even unfortunate things that happen, you might discover much of what you stress over isn't really worth the energy. Make no mistake, college is serious – it forms the foundation for many things in your life. At times, taking things too seriously forces you to lose the perspective you need to maintain a healthy balance.

Benefits of Laughing it Off:

- Reduces stress: The physical benefits of laughter are well documented; it positively affects your breathing and releases the "happy" endorphins which help you maintain a positive attitude.
- Gives you back perspective: If you perceive something as "kind of funny" it allows you to "not sweat the small stuff."
- Connects you to others: When you share the funny things that happen with others, and they reciprocate, it becomes clear you are not alone.

KNOW YOUR HEALTH INSURANCE INFORMATION.

Many students going off to college are familiar with the need to have health insurance. Whether you are covered under your parents' policy, employer or state program, you must have health insurance and be up to date with all of the required immunizations. If you don't have coverage, check with your office of admissions or health center. You will need to show proof of coverage to register for classes. Be sure to also know the limitations of whatever policy you are under and what identification is needed so you'll have the proper paperwork when necessary. Be sure to always carry your health insurance card on you. To help you collect this vital data, take a moment to complete the following – it can be one of the smartest things you ever do!

Information of Interest:

My health insurance is carried by: _____

_____

Their contact number is: _____

_____

The policy is under this name: _____

_____

My account/policy number is: _____

_____

A copy of this policy is located: _____

_____

SCHEDULE YOUR ANNUAL MEDICAL EXAMS IN ADVANCE.

Just as regular check-ups keep your car running, regular visits to your doctors and other health care providers keep you healthy. Be proactive. Maintain your health by maintaining annual appointments with your doctors. This is a better strategy than trying to schedule last minute annual visits with your dentist, primary care physician, and eye doctor, for instance. Don't let the busy nature of your life mean you delay these visits for four years!

Once you know your academic demands and schedules at the beginning of each year start making phone calls and schedule your annual appointments. Most of your professors will provide syllabi with important dates and your college or university will publish their academic calendar, usually years in advance. A good strategy is to make all of your appointments during the same week each year.

If you attend school far from home you might want to find a local doctor. Contact your campus health center or insurance carrier for recommendations. Both will be able to tell you about quality health care in the area and identify those in your network.

LET PROFESSORS (AND OTHER IMPORTANT PEOPLE) KNOW WHEN YOU ARE SICK.

When we don't feel well, we sometimes feel like the whole world can tell. Unfortunately, this is not true. When your physical health is weakened, you really are the only one who knows something is wrong. From this point on, you need to demonstrate self-respect by communicating with those who need to know you're not feeling well. Your communication skills in college become more important than ever; no one is going come around to "check up" on you.

You might ask, "Why in the world would my professor care about whether or not I don't feel well?" If you don't show up for class your professor would probably appreciate knowing it was for a legitimate reason and not because you were "blowing them off." They might be more inclined to help you out with missed materials, or appreciate the opportunity to remind you of course policies with regards to absence or materials not turned in. Make sure your sickness doesn't impact your success by communicating appropriately.

Living with others can be good and bad. When you are not feeling your best, those relationships become intensified. If you don't communicate with your roommates, they'll go on with business as usual. For example, you may have a tremendous head cold and be trying to take a nap. Your unsuspecting roommates come home from class wanting to let loose. If you've communicated with them about feeling sick, they are more likely to adjust their behavior to let you rest. Similarly, you may be struggling with a personal problem and need some space. If they know this, they'll not only be able to leave you alone, but might check in to see if you need them!

Even if you live at home while attending college, you probably won't see your family as much as given your workload and necessary study time. If you are going away to school, you probably won't see them as much because of your workload and the distance. Either way, you should think about how to communicate with your parents or family when you don't feel well. You certainly don't want to alarm them, but if you feel it's important they know your current health status, fill them in. Don't assume the health office, doctor or hospital contacted anyone on your behalf. The federal privacy act (FERPA) prevents them from disclosing your status without your permission or can only do so when you are a potential harm to yourself or others. While you might want to be independent and have waited many years for your privacy, think about keeping those who care about you in the loop.

Chapter 24

NOW FACTOR EIGHTEEN

JUST BECAUSE YOU CAN DOESN'T MEAN YOU SHOULD

"Choose your friends. Be around people who are positive and will lift you up when you get down. Find the ones who make you a better person."

Hope Smith, student
Texas Woman's University, Denton, Texas

DECIDE HOW TO MAKE DECISIONS.

You are a talented person or you wouldn't be a college student. With these aptitudes come many choices. The many skills and abilities you possess (yet may not recognize) translate into endless possibilities in college and beyond. Don't think so? Take a moment and in one of the "Random Thought" areas, write the heading, "I'm Good at These Things."

Your responses are important. They are your assets and beginning steps in creating a life filled with happiness. Keep in mind, just because you *are* good at something doesn't mean you *should* spend your college years and the rest of your life doing it, especially if it doesn't make you happy. Being good at numbers, yet disliking working with numbers, illustrates this point. How do you decide?

STRATEGY FOR MAKING DECISIONS:

1. Figure out what you do best and ask yourself what brings you happiness.
2. Look for ways these two things intersect.
3. Make lists of what it would take to do what makes you happy.
4. Identify the potential risks involved, including expenses, resources, time and so on.
5. Determine what you are willing to give up in order to get what you want.

To not have a clue, is a clue. That's part of the reason you are in college; to clarify the ways in which you want to spend your life.

GET INTO A HEALTHY SLEEPING ROUTINE.

To do anything well, even things you find easy, requires mental and physical health. Having ample rest assures you the stamina and energy to do everything you want to do. Are you going to get eight hours of solid sleep each night as a college student? Maybe that's not completely realistic, but you need to keep your body on a routine because a lack of sleep is one thing that will catch up with you!

Some people simply need more sleep than others. Figure out what you need to maintain your activities and your mood throughout the day and try to get that amount of sleep on a consistent basis. Take a nap during the day if you are exhausted. Drinking caffeinated beverages, or eating spicy foods in the evening may contribute to poor sleeping patterns, too. One of the surest ways not to sleep during class is to sleep during the night!

Do your best to create the relaxing environment you need to be able to unwind and fall asleep. If your neighbors are making noise you may have to become more assertive by letting them know you need them to quiet down so you can sleep. While this is easier said than done, most residence halls have "quiet hours" wherein residents are expected to "keep it down." Be sure to let folks know what you need; you might be surprised at how they'll respect you. Reciprocate!

RESIST THE TEMPTATION TO GO HOME EVERY WEEKEND.

"Home" can mean different things to different people. Sometimes it's better to be "away." Sometimes being home brings back wonderful memories of friends, and favorite familiar places. If you like going home, and could go home every weekend, should you? No.

Give college a chance. How will you ever know how terrific it can be? Much of the fun and making of friendships happens on the weekends when there's more time to relax. If you're never there during those times, you will miss out on campus events, hang time, and meals that never end. These are times when people really get to know each other. Not going home on weekends allows you to explore your college's town, visit friends at other colleges, and meet people who come to your campus to visit. Make a life for yourself on campus, catch up on reading, studying and homework, and strengthen your new friendships by doing fun things you don't have time to do during the week

Don't spend money you don't have.

College students have no money. That's the rule. Not having money makes you creative. Whether you have no money or some money, now is the time to start taking better ownership of your financial future. Although charge cards were meant to make shopping for things easier and reduce paying until the end of the month, problems arise when you buy more than you can afford!

Credit card interest rates which average 18%, 21%, or 24% can get you into big trouble quickly, especially if you can't pay them off in full every month. During college, attempt to budget and stay within your budget. You can prevent problems with finance and interest charges, for example, if you maintain a low credit card limit of $300 or $500 to access in the case of emergencies, or for things more difficult to pay for with cash like airline tickets and books bought online. Buying things to "cheer you up" only gets you in more trouble.

To keep your payments down, make them on time or you'll get sacked with a late fee which can be hefty. Worse, the late payment will appear in your credit history and could lower your credit rating; your credit rating is important because this numerical score indicates to a lender whether you are a good credit risk or not. When you're looking to buy a car and finance it, your score will not only determine if you are eligible to get the loan, but at what interest rate. Generally, a high credit rating means you get access to better interest rates; you pay less than someone with a low score.

The only bills you have are the ones you create! Do you need to treat everyone to pizza? Is a new shirt all that important to your wardrobe? If you don't have the money, you don't have the money. Whether it's credit card interest, school loans or anticipating your car needing repairs, whenever you can spend less or not at all, you win! This brings up the habit of saving money, or paying your future first.

You can't save what you don't have either! Whenever you do find yourself with "some" money, get into a responsible habit of saving it. In fact, save whatever you can as often as you can! Ten dollars a week may not seem like much, but over the course of a school year it becomes $400.00, or enough to go on a ski weekend next February (the one you missed this year because you couldn't afford it!) You can also use "saved" money to pay down any credit card balances. To keep you motivate to save, remember this Chinese Proverb, "The art is not in making money, but in keeping it."

TAKE OWNERSHIP FOR YOUR FINANCIAL FUTURE.

By putting yourself on a monthly budget you avoid spending haphazardly. As you grow in responsibility, you grow in the need to control the allocation of your resources. This is your financial future, as well as an investment in how you learn to take care of money and support your priorities in life.

Never put yourself on a monthly budget? Take a moment

right now and estimate your income and expenses for the year. How much will you take in from available sources (INCOME) and how much will you need to spend for all of your obligations (EXPENSES)? Total up each section and then subtract the Expense amount from the INCOME amount (A-B).

MONTHLY INCOME	TOTAL AMOUNT SPENT MONTHLY
Parents	
Loans	
Scholarships	
Working	
Financial Aid	
Miscellaneous Income	
INCOME SUBTOTAL (A)	
MONTHLY EXPENSES	
Rent/Room & Board	
Utilities (Gas, Electric, Cable)	
Telephone	
Groceries	
Car Payment/Transportation	
Insurance	
Gasoline/Oil	
Entertainment (movies, shows)	
Eating Out/Vending	
Tuition	
Books	
School Fees	

Computer Expenses	
Miscellaneous Expenses	
EXPENSES SUBTOTAL (B)	
NET INCOME (A-B)	

Source: ABOUT.COM

How did your balance come out next to "NET INCOME?" Is the number positive or negative? Hopefully you have what you need. This table is not meant to scare you; quite the contrary, it is meant to get you in touch with reality. If the balance is positive, you'll be able to meet your expenses as estimated. If the balance is negative, you'll need to figure out ways to cut costs or increase income in order to meet your obligations. If you don't have it, you can't spend it. How can you support a negative balance?

LOOK ON AND OFF CAMPUS FOR A JOB.

Loans. Taking out loans to cover college costs is a common practice. The dilemma arises when you take out more loans than necessary. Are you willing to work during the summer, and especially during the academic year to avoid loans? When you prefer to spend more than you can afford on non-essential items, you need to find income other than loans. Borrowed money should not go for concert tickets or designer shoes! *Essential expenses* are those which support the pursuit of your degree, and cover basic living expenses.

If you need to work as most college students do, find a working schedule that allows you to attend classes and still be a part of college life. On your campus, there may be work not dependent on qualifying for financial aid. The key is to be assertive and find out in person, if jobs are available. Check out offices who frequently hire students like admissions, student activities, or dining services.

Career services maintains off-campus job listings. Try the job postings in the local newspaper, too. Often community members, even faculty, are looking for responsible help.

Always ask the tough questions, "Do I need everything I spend money on?" "What could I stop doing or buying to lower my monthly expenses?" You probably can get by having a little less in order to be more financially responsible. Tap into your sense of self-discipline. Start now practicing how to make wise choices about your spending and you'll live a life of prosperity!

BALANCE YOUR CHECKBOOK.

The simplest math, yet college students resist knowing exact-ly how much money is in their account. Are you in the "red" or "black" or will you know when the bank sends you a pink slip? *Balancing your checkbook* is reconciling (or accounting) for what you say you have and what the bank says you have in your account. Since you are not above making a mistake recording entries in your checkbook register, and your bank is not above making the occasional error, balancing helps to insure accuracy on both sides. A helpful strategy is to reserve the first Monday of every month to sit down and pay bills, review your budget and reconcile your accounts.

Balancing your checkbook also means you know how much money you have available to you at any time. Successful balancing of your checkbook relies on two things; entering everything you spend in your register and matching your statement to what you have entered. Given electronic banking, balancing your checkbook is easier than ever. A great strategy is to plug your account into Microsoft Excel© and download your banking transactions directly from your bank. This makes it easy to reconcile and balance your checkbook every month. You know what you've got!

START BUILDING YOUR INVESTMENT PORTFOLIO NOW.

Smart students live within their means. Even smarter students invest! Learn now about money management and investing strategies. Why not take a course on the subject as an elective? Attend financial workshops and seminars. Although you may not have much money to invest, learning what you need to know now will set you up for a healthy financial future. The more you know, the less intimidated you'll feel about investing. Time is on your side.

Compound interest is earning money on what your money earns. If you invested two dollars a day and got only a 5% return, you'd have over $25,000 before you were forty (Source: ncnblog.com.) If you invested $1000 at the age of 21 and never touched it, by retirement at 65 years of age, you'd have over a million! Think about turning what you'd spend on a venti caramel latte each day into a small fortune. You are in control of your destiny when you control your finances.

GO WITHOUT A CAR.

You may be used to having access to a car or having your own car; however, if you're living on campus why do you need one? Everything you need to be successful probably exists right on campus. Hard to imagine, but there are negatives to having a car on campus if you really don't need one.

THE DOWNSIDE OF HAVING A CAR:

- Gas prices
- Where to park it
- Getting to and from the lots where your car will be allowed
- People wanting to borrow it
- People needing rides

- Facing temptations to drive home, the ice cream shop, etc.
- Issues associated with drinking and driving
- Costs of maintaining it (oil change, car wash)

Commuting students need a mode of transportation. Public transportation is one option if it's available. The good news for commuting students is that parking is available in "commuter lots." Some colleges have additional parking fees to guarantee your space, while others operate on a first-come first-serve basis. With climbing gas prices, car pooling is a great alternative. Look for adds in the school paper or ask around.

Chapter 25

NOW FACTOR NINETEEN

COLLEGE IS THE REAL WORLD

"I can't think of anything more dangerous than following the crowd."

Phil Bernard, Associate Dean of Students
Wentworth Institute of Technology, Boston, Massachusetts

Find a Mentor.

Who is the first person you would call for support and advice? Is it a coach, employer, teacher, parent, sibling, or grandparent? Whose opinion do you trust to guide you in the right direction? These kinds of people are called "mentors," and you always should have one, regardless of your age.

No one ever said you were meant to walk through life alone or without someone to help guide you through this ever-changing world. A *mentor* is a support system; someone who believes in you, is honest with you, is there for you, directs you where to go and is a role model whose opinion you value. Typically older than you, a mentor may be someone in the same career you wish to pursue, or who has taken a path you would like to be on. They help you get there!

You may already have a mentor, but there is nothing wrong with finding more than one! Take a moment while you are in college to connect with someone you feel represents who you want to be when you grow up. Ask them to serve as your "mentor."

Network and follow up with people.

In some way or form, you are part of a network. Various social medias make it easy to connect with something or someone based on what you have in common. The classroom, dorm room or locker room, are places where you can cast your net.

Networks are connections of individuals who maintain mutually supportive relationships. Each member gives and takes, while maintaining the obligation to always follow up and stay in communication. You must follow up! Talking to one person often leads to meeting his or her friends. To meet people, you have to get out there. You have to join something. Remember to show up after your sign up, or you will miss the benefits of enlarging your social circle. Don't count on existing group members to introduce themselves to you. Jump out of your comfort zone and extend your hand!

As you begin to grow your network, keep a journal of who you meet and always ask for their contact information or business card. Follow up by inviting them to lunch or coffee. Find out what matters most to those you meet and what makes them unique. Write it down. You just never know where a new contact will lead you!

REGISTER TO VOTE.

Have you ever voted in an election? Whether voting for the student government president, state senator, or president of the United States, your vote counts. The issues of elections are driven by those going to the polls to vote. When college students fail to exercise their right to vote, candidates run on platforms popular to those who do vote. A quick call to your hometown town hall or board of elections (or quick search on the web,) gets you the information needed to register to vote in local, state and federal elections. There is often a significant lead time to register, so put this on a TO DO list and get it done now. You can choose to be part of history, or watch it pass you by.

Don't forget campus elections! Your vote is your voice with campus elections, too. For example, do you know how your tuition dollars are being spent? Start by knowing *who* is spending them on your behalf. Your student government (often called, "SGA") is charged with dividing up a significant amount of resources, you have a right to influence where this money goes.

When you vote, you can make a difference and effectuate. When you don't, you let others (usually those considerably older who do go to the polls) take control over what kind of Social Security benefits you will have, who will determine your liberties, the kind of health care you will be able to afford, and even how you define, "marriage." Be smart and cast your vote. You can register to vote at www.rockthevote.com and begin to be a part of change. Being in college is being in the real world. Vote.

Chapter 26

NOW FACTOR TWENTY

THE FUTURE IS YOURS TO CREATE

"A student is successful when they take on the role of architect and designer of their own college experience. Successful students know; like in building a home, a strong foundation is only the beginning of the tasks at hand. Seeking ways to enhance the educational experience through intentional design is what makes college a place where students can thrive."

Cindy Kane, Director of the Office of Student Involvement & Leadership
Bridgewater State College, Massachusetts

THINK BEYOND GETTING A "JOB."

When asked, "Why are you going to college?" nine out of ten students will reply, "To get a job." When you change the way you think about a "job" (which coincidently could stand for "just over broke,") the pressure to know what you will be doing for the rest of your life goes away. Now is a great time to think beyond a "job" and explore how you want to make a difference in the world. Where are your talents and interests best suited?

A *job* is a task an individual performs in exchange for compensation – it is often a means to an ends, where the number one goal is to make money. In many situations, you exchange your time and energy for a paycheck and without compensation, you would quit! There just isn't the passion or interest to sustain you. When you have significant expenses, like school or car loans, it makes sense to "get a job." However, as a college student, try to expand how you think about your future after graduation. If you could do anything, what would that be? Travel? Volunteer? Go to graduate school? Join AmeriCorps?

Keep your eyes wide open in the years ahead. Explore a variety of subject areas and take full advantage of the numerous electives at your disposal. You may find yourself interested in something entirely new, something you'd never considered pursuing as a career.

PICK A CAREER THAT ENGAGES YOU.

So what is a "career?" A *career* is a specific profession or occupation that requires special education and/or training. It is a field or industry you train for to increase competency and proficiency, and often requires advancing your education or additional certification to advance. Given the cumulative nature of a career, each step is meant to be enjoyed while setting you up for the next exciting challenge and opportunity for growth.

Unfortunately, people end up in careers chosen for them by well meaning loved ones such as parents, grandparents, spouses, significant others, teachers, school counselors and so on. Do yourself a favor and never allow anyone to push you into a career because *they* believe you would be great in that profession.

Similar to having a "job" for the wrong reasons, it's hard to sustain long term motivation in a profession or occupation that does not engage, excite and stimulate you. When this happens, it's time to alter your course. There's nothing wrong with changing careers. Many adults around you have changed their careers 4 to 6 times already! If your career choice does not allow you to experience a personal sense of satisfaction, why continue to pursue it? College is a laboratory of career exploration. Time to put on your lab coat!

WHEN SELECTING A CAREER ASK YOURSELF THESE THREE QUESTIONS:

Do I have a high-level of interest for this profession or
   field of study?
Do I have a medium-level of interest for this profession or
   field of study?
Do I have a low-level of interest for this profession or field
   of study?

Avoid selecting a career before you are ready, or because you can make lots of money. Just because a profession is considered "hot and booming" doesn't make it a good fit either. Trusting you'll be guaranteed a job upon graduation, however, makes sense if you have loans to pay off. But when seeking to live your passion and get paid for it, put thought into professions and occupations allowing you to be fully engaged.

VISIT THE IDEA OF VOCATION.

Do you hear your name being called? It may seem easier at this point in life to think of your future by considering the pursuit of a "vocation," as opposed to a "career." In Latin, *voco* means "to call." *Vocation* is work you are called to perform while living your best life on Mother Earth. You are drawn or pulled to your vocation. In many cases, your vocation picks you.

KINDS OF CALLINGS:

- Are you called to teach?
- Are you called to write and author books?
- Are you called to sing, write and/or compose inspirational and entertaining music?
- Are you called to manage and lead within for profit, non-profit, government and/or social service and community-based organizations?
- Are you called to create artistic creations?
- Are you called to a healthcare profession of some sort?
- Are you called to protect and service the larger community as a police officer, fire fighter or military professional?
- Are you called to help heal the hurting and abused by way of counseling and therapy?
- Are you called to spiritually and religiously lead, educate and inform the masses?
- Are you called to motivate and inspire the helpless and hopeless?

An ultimate goal of college should be to start discovering your personal calling. One way to begin is by identifying your personal and professional Talents, Abilities, Gifts and Skills (referred to by Jermaine M. Davis as T.A.G.S) – these are both natural born strengths and cultivated strengths that manifest and develop over a period of time. Your T.A.G.S. are the strengths that are easiest for you to perform; they are the talents and areas in life, school and work where you naturally excel. Your T.A.G.S. allow you to standout, be noticed, and get recognized.

EXAMPLES OF YOUR T.A.G.S.:

- Listening T.A.G.S.
- Interpersonal Communication and Relations T.A.G.S.
- Pay Attention to Details and Organizational T.A.G.S.
- Creative, Entrepreneurial and Innovative T.A.G.S.
- Critical Analysis and Critical Thinking T.A.G.S.
- Culinary Art T.A.G.S.
- Medical and Science T.A.G.S.
- Technology T.A.G.S.
- Musical and Artistic T.A.G.S.
- Project Management T.A.G.S.

THINKING PAD

Question to Ask: If money wasn't an issue, what profession or calling interests me most?

_____
_____
_____
_____
_____
_____

Question to Ask: What kind of work gets me super duper excited? What do I love to do?

_____
_____
_____
_____
_____
_____

Question to Ask: What is my unique competitive advantage? What differentiates me from everyone else?

Question to Ask: What consistent compliments have I received from others? Where have I been a superstar in life, school and work?

BELIEVE IN YOURSELF.

You were once a kid. You ran in circles, played with strangers and invited anyone into your sandbox. You were filled with curiosity, hope and energy. Enough was never enough when you are young. You always wanted the babysitter to read one more story, the birthday kid to give you another slice of cake (after all, you brought the best present to the party) and the treat of staying up an extra hour!

Now that you are all "grown up" and being described as an "emerging adult" or "non-traditional student" you have to make a concerted effort to hold onto the child that's within you! Your life is more complicated and feels more like work than play; that's because you are in college and it is suppose to be more work than play.

By reminding yourself that the process of play actually helps you work, you will discover the logic in being adventurous and kid-like. Seek ways of experiencing joy when you feel sad. Engage in silliness when you are getting all stressed out. Make faces in the mirror when you are taking yourself too seriously. Most importantly, talk to yourself…out loud! Say affirming phrases to yourself. When in doubt, believe in you!

Question to Ask: What games did you play as a child that brought you joy?

_____

_____

_____

_____

_____

Question to Ask: What's the greatest compliment you enjoy receiving because it validates who you want to be?

_____

_____

_____

_____

_____

Question to Ask: If you were playing "hide and go seek," what is your favorite hiding place in your head?

_____

_____

_____

_____

_____

Question to Ask: You made it this far in life, who has been your biggest fan?

_____

_____

_____

_____

- -

Question to Ask: What characteristics of your very being keep you going when you feel like giving up?

_____

_____

_____

_____

- -

Chapter 27

TAKE CARE NOW

"Find your place – a place that is for you! It could be a physical location where you are particularly comfortable, or it could be with a group of students with whom you have things in common. But, find your place – any place – where you can be who you are."

Leslie Heusted, Director of the Danforth University Center Washington University of St. Louis, Missouri

Is a line a shape? Now is your chance to guess again using the answer you didn't use the first time. You had a fifty percent chance of getting it right or wrong at the beginning of this book, and the odds haven't changed. There was no penalty or prize either way. Is a line a shape?

We have tried to suggest throughout this book that some answers in life are relative, while others are absolutes. In the years ahead, you will come to understand which type of answers will serve you best. Will you say, "It doesn't matter" when dealing with what's morally right or wrong? Will you say, "Sorry, I've never done this before and I've messed up," when acknowledging your bad decision and determination to forgive yourself and move on?

Which Now Factors are you going to prioritize and take to heart first? You are encouraged to appreciate these "absolutes" and "observations" sooner, not later! By quickly adding yourself to the Formula for College Success, you navigate your new environment better than "winging it." Here's another look at your potential future.

THE FORMULA FOR COLLEGE SUCCESS

College Success = f (P + E) + Now Factors

It's time to plug yourself into the equation and become an official "college student." By now, you should be better equipped to literally "do the math" and start enjoying this exciting, yet challenging time. College is work – hard work! Use this privilege as an opportunity to continue becoming an incredible individual who will make the world a better place, just by being in it!

Begin sharing your talents and enjoying the simple things around you. Remember to pat yourself on the back once in awhile! All the craziness shakes out eventually leaving you with what you need.

At your graduation, you will realize how much you didn't know about succeeding in college when you began. You will smile as you hear someone speak of all you've done to get to this place in your life. Maybe this will be some famous person, like a Nobel Peace Prize winner. Maybe it will be a classmate or relative. Maybe it will be a voice in your own head acknowledging the many positive outcomes of your efforts. You did it!

In the meantime, stay focused on the purpose of higher education; to create a better you equipped to work towards the greater social good! And, in case you are still wondering… a line *is* a shape.

ABOUT THE AUTHORS

Jermaine M. Davis

Jermaine M. Davis is an award winning Professor of Communication Studies at Century College, the largest community college in the State of Minnesota. Jermaine is founder and CEO of two companies: Seminars & Workshops, Inc. and Snack Attack Vending of Minnesota. Jermaine holds an MA in Speech Communication and an MA in Education. He is a recent graduate of Cornell University's Diversity Management Certificate Program. Jermaine is the author and coauthor of six books including: *Get Up Off Your Butt & Do It NOW!*, *Leading with Greatness*, *Be Diversity Competent* and the *Stand Out Women's Quote Journal Leadership Series*.

After growing up on the west side of Chicago's housing projects and losing six family members to violent deaths, Jermaine was inspired to become a professional speaker and an inspirational teacher. He is one of the country's most requested speakers and college entertainers, delivering over 100 presentations annually to both college and corporate audiences. In the college market, Jermaine is known as a presenter who is engaging, enthusiastic and entertaining while delivering life changing messages. Most importantly, Jermaine loves helping college students become future leaders. He is fully committed to helping individuals discover their life purpose and become successful in life, school & work.

To use Jermaine as a keynote speaker, workshop leader or to purchase one of his books you can contact him at:

651.487.7576
www.jermainedavis.com
jermaine@jermainedavis.com

Nancy Hunter Denney

Nancy Hunter Denney is a nationally recognized author and inspirational educator with a passion for life and leadership. In 1993, after living everyone else's definition of having it all, she resigned from administrative duties at a private engineering college to raise her own children, spend more time with her husband, start her own speaking business, and pursue her true passions in life. Nancy specializes in inspiring those who make a difference, especially non-profit helping organizations and is known for her high energy presentation style, sense of humor and passionate delivery of original content. She has appeared on over 900 college and university campuses and is a frequent keynote speaker at national, regional and state conferences in higher education, women's leadership and non-profit helping organizations. On the national stage she has appeared with Dr. Phil, Soledad O'Brien, Dana Reeves, Sarah Weddington, Amanda Gore and has enjoyed inspiring corporate clients ranging from Deloitte-Touche to Century 21.

Nancy is the president of Zing! Leadership Development Systems, LLC. She has authored two books, and coauthored three books on life and leadership. Her publishing company is dedicated to helping inspiring authors see their ideas come to life.

The parent of two college students, Nancy resides in Marion, Massachusetts where she also assumes the roles of wife, business owner and first mate.

Nancy is the author of numerous books, including:

Zing! 21 Insights on Maximizing Your Influence.
2nd Edition. Massachusetts: Zing! Leadership Development Systems, LLC. 2008

Lessons from the Road: Inspirational Insights by Leading Speakers in Education. Massachusetts: Zing! Leadership Development Systems, LLC publisher. 2007

Let Your Leadership Speak: How to Lead and Be Heard. Massachusetts: Future Productions. 2000

Life by Design: A Do-It-Yourself Approach to Achieving Happiness. Massachusetts: Victory Publications. 1997

For product information or to inquire about the speaking services of Nancy Hunter Denney:

Nancy Hunter Denney
Box 1041
Marion, MA 02738

508.864.4027
www.nancyhunterdenney.com
nhdenney@aol.com

Michael Miller

Passion. Energy. Enthusiasm. These attributes are what propel your organization toward achieving its goals. Whether yours is a department in a large organization or a club at a small college, your staff needs drive to get their job done. Inspired individuals will work to get what they want – and help others to do the same. Sometimes, these individuals need a source of energy and motivation to draw from – as source who can empower them to see what they can accomplish. When your group lacks energy, where do you turn to sustain them?

Michael Miller. He's passionate and bold…and he won't let go of you until you learn the ways to get what you want out of your time, life and work. Whatever your organization's needs, Michael uses his energy and enthusiasm to get your group totally focused on the topic. Always humorous and sometimes wild, Michael insists on getting your audience completely involved, inspiring open communication that brings about positive change for participants. Audiences appreciate his raspy voice and are drawn to his gestures; however, it is his intensity that stays with them and motivates them to achieve their goals.

Whether he's with you for a day-long workshop or a week-long "Leader-in-Residence" consulting program, Michael will get full participation. Participants trust him immediately because of his forward blend of humor and intense caring. This creates an immediate rapport of trust – that both attracts and challenges participants.

To contact or book Michael Miller:

Fun Enterprises
781.340.0180
www.reallymotivated.com

Zing!™ Leadership Development Systems, LLC

Zing!™ Leadership Development Systems, LLC was created to provide assistance in the development of creative, impactful and inspiring leadership curriculum and resources based around the Zing! approach to teaching, living and learning leadership. A variety of inspirational products are available through the online store. Recent additions to the LLC include a publishing division for aspiring authors with a positive message to share.

Contact Information:

Box 1041
Marion, MA 02738
508.864.4027
www.zingleadership.com
nhdenney@aol.com